Who, Me?!

Are You Weak, Small and Foolish Enough to REALLY Be Used by God?

---

by

John Enlow

DEDICATION

First, I dedicate this book to the Holy Spirit; the Promise sent from the Father has truly been special in my life. To the degree I have been able to open areas of my life to Him, to that degree He has continued to transform me. May He breathe upon this book so that it goes beyond the impact of mere words. May He be exalted, honored and given more room to operate through the influence of this book. Thank You, Jesus, for sending us such an awesome Teacher, Comforter, Counselor and Friend!

Second, I must dedicate this book to my wife, Elizabeth. She has walked with me through so many phases of my spiritual journey and has been a constant encouragement for me. Her proddings and her direct assistance in finding the time to do this whole project have been invaluable. She also served as my first proofreader, and her input and excitement as she read what I had written was a great help to me. She has consistently carried the challenge of raising and home-schooling our children, and during the preparation of this book, she has been obliged to carry this important responsibility alone, for the most part. At key times during the development of the book, she also received some clear direction from the Lord that helped give me confidence for the next step. In a very true way, this book is really a joint product of the two of us. Thanks a lot, Honey. I love you!

ACKNOWLEDGMENTS

First, I would like to acknowledge my parents, Jack and Gladys Enlow. Their abandoned pursuit of God has been an awesome example to me and to our entire family. Even now, in their seventies and with some serious illnesses, they are serving the Lord on the mission field in Peru. They took us through church situations that even they regret, but they were always pure in heart, desiring only deeper levels of communion with the Lord. Their unwavering faith in the Lord through every conceivable type of test is a lasting testament to their lives. Their scores of spiritual sons and daughters assure them of a rich reward in the hereafter.

I must thank David and Stephanie Palusky for their ongoing encouragement and help during the process of the writing of this book. For years, David asked me, "When are you going to write?" They were both on many of the missionary trips described in this book and witnessed with me the acts that God performed.

I must also thank the dozens of other people who have been part of our missionary teams. Thanks for your part in adding to the stories I tell here. I surely will forget someone, but I must name some of the ordinary Joes whom God has mightily used: Frank, Scott, Vicki, Steve, Suzanne, Danny, Nathan, Sharon, Steven, Bobby, Kathy, Jim, Robby, Angie, Andy, Stephanie, Karen, David, Jessica, Eddie, Greg, Mike, Stan, Woody, Jodie, Brian, Wing See, Sara, Jerry, Tom, Sandy, Mickey, Paul, Bobby — and all the rest of you. Thank you! It never has been a one-man operation. May this book bless you also as you remember what God has done.

CONTENTS

For you see your calling, brethren, that not many wise according to the flesh, not many mighty, not many noble, are called. But God has chosen the foolish things of the world to put to shame the wise, and God has chosen the weak things of the world to put to shame the things which are mighty; and the base things of the world and the things which are despised God has chosen, and the things which are not, to bring to nothing the things that are, that no flesh should glory in His presence.

1 Corinthians 1:26-29

INTRODUCTION

God is on the move! Fires of renewal and revival are increasing exponentially all across the world. It is time for God's people to come out of their caves and to make themselves available to carry His glory to "the ends of the earth." It is time to stop disqualifying ourselves from being part of this end-time army of God. All hands aboard! This is the cry of the Spirit to His Church.

There is a cry going forth from the depths of the heart of God to the depths of the heart of every single believer. The harvest is ripe, and He needs laborers. It is time to stop determining through our own self-evaluation just how much God can really use us. Let the Lord of the Harvest make those determinations. We carry deep and distorted assumptions of what an "anointed" person really looks like, and we all too often assume that it just cannot be someone who appears as "ordinary" as we do. We must cast off such assumptions, for they are the only thing that can truly disqualify us during this exciting time in the history of the Church. If we know God, we can do great exploits in His name.

Satan may have informed you that, for whatever reason, your ability to be used by God is limited or nonexistent. He is telling saints everywhere that they just don't have what it takes to really be used by God in any significant way. He hopes to lock us into mediocrity based on our perceptions of our own lack of giftedness.

Whatever the level of your Christian experience, this book is for you. If you are in a state of communion and intimacy with God, then you have not been disqualified from carrying God's power and glory. You may even discover that you're a vessel that the Lord would really PREFER to empower.

For some reason, we twenty-first century Christians have determined that theological training, charisma and oratorical skills are what most qualify a person to do the REALLY important things in the Kingdom of God. But nothing could be further from the truth, and this is made clear in the Scriptures. Often a one-time confrontation with the truth of God's Word is not enough to overcome our preconceived ideas and work that truth into our spirits. There is a need for truth to be reinforced through multiple scriptures, examples and testimonies. This we will do here.

In the pages of this book, we will take a new look at the "mighty men" whom God chose to use — men like Moses, Gideon, Paul, David, and even Jesus. As you see these men in a very different light, with all their faults and failures and limitations made evident, my hope is that it will cause you to see yourself in a new light as well — as one whom God can use. This will begin a process of transformation in the core of your being that can lead you to a new level of achievement in God's Kingdom.

The book is not just about men and women "of old." In these pages, we will also examine very ordinary men and women of today and learn what God is doing through their lives. They are painters, pressure washers, hole diggers, carpenters, housewives, teachers and businessmen, and they are being used by God to perform exploits in many nations. Entire cities and nations are now being affected by "nobodies."

If you are a "nobody" with a great love for God, this book will ignite some unquenchable fires in your spirit, and I believe that you will never be the same. As you read these pages, I believe you will sense the Lord releasing new faith, new hope, and a new vision into your spirit. I believe that a work of impartation will take place for you that will change your life forever.

As you read, you may find yourself asking, *Who, Me?!* And you may be surprised by the answer you receive.

John Enlow
Loganville, Georgia

CHAPTER 1

GOD HAS CHOSEN THE FOOLISH THINGS

Because the foolishness of God is wiser than men, and the weakness of God is stronger than men. For you see your calling, brethren, that not many wise according to the flesh, not many mighty, not many noble, are called. But God has chosen the foolish things of the world to put to shame the wise, and God has chosen the weak things of the world to put to shame the things which are mighty; and the base things of the world and the things which are despised God has chosen, and the things which are not, to bring to nothing the things that are, that no flesh should glory in His presence.
1 Corinthians 1:25-29

Who does God really prefer to use to advance the issues of His Kingdom? After studying the Scriptures and Church history, we may all acknowledge that over the years God has used every imaginable type of person. However, I want to set forth the question: Who does God *prefer* to use? The answer to this question that we find in the Scriptures is not in any way vague. It is, rather, very clear. His preference is to greatly use *the weak, small and foolish*.

For many Christians, the words of 1 Corinthians 1:25-29 are well-known. However, let us take a second look at them, to see if something new will stand out to us this time.

For instance, verse 26 points out something that we must not overlook. Not many *"wise,"* not many *"mighty,"* and not many *"noble"* are even *"called."* This word "called" in the original Greek is the word *kletos* and means "invited." So what it is clearly saying is that not many wise, mighty or noble are even *invited* by the Lord. If that thought puts a "burr" under our saddle, it may be a sign that there is something to be learned here.

9

In verse 27, we read: *"But God has chosen ... ."* Let's stop there for a moment and look at this word *"chosen."* As we know, our English New Testament was translated from an original Greek manuscript. In the original Greek, the word translated "chosen" is *eklegomai,* meaning "to select," "to choose as favorite," (with the implication of first choice). So, before we continue, let us give these first words their proper weight. We are talking about God's original intention — a purposeful choice. When verse 27 says, *"But God has chosen the foolish things of the world to put to shame the wise"* (NIV), it reveals His original intent. Seeing the meaning of the original Greek really brings the true meaning of this passage home to us.

If God has *chosen* that which is *foolish,* just what kind of foolishness is He talking about? The Greek word used here is *moros,* and it is a very interesting one. The first two definitions of *moros* are "dull" and "stupid." Another definition is " blockhead," and another is "absurd." As some might have already guessed, it is from this word that we derive our English word "moron."

If that's what God means by *foolish,* what does He mean by *wise* in the same verse? This word is translated from the Greek word *sophos.* This word is the root of our English word "sophisticated." So God has chosen the morons of this world over the sophisticated.

That's not all. Not only has God chosen morons over those who are sophisticated, but He has also chosen to *"shame the wise"* through preferring *"foolish things."* The Greek word translated here as "shame" is *kataischuno.* It is a strong word that means more than shame. It means "to bring to shame, to disgrace, to confound or totally embarrass to the point of making one to blush." That's powerful!

The rest of verse 27 says, *"And God has chosen the weak things of the world to put to shame the things that are mighty."* This statement is very similar to the first statement. Once again, we can feel the impact of the words by looking up their original Greek meanings. The Greek word translated here as "weak" is *asthenes,* meaning "strengthless, more feeble, impotent, sick, weaker, weakness, or weak thing." The Greek word translated "mighty" is *ischuros.* This word means "boisterous, powerful, strong, valiant, forceful." So God has intentionally chosen the feeble to totally embarrass the forceful.

In case someone hasn't yet gotten the picture, Paul continues this line of thinking in verse 28, when he says, *"And the base things of this world and the things which are despised God has chosen."* The word translated here as "base" is another great Greek word: *agenes*. It is difficult to define *agenes* in a single word. It is made up of two parts. The first part is *a,* meaning "being absent or having none." Our word amoral, meaning having no morals, uses this speech formation. The second part of *agenes* — *genes* — is just what it looks like in English. *Agenes,* then, literally means "having no genetic nobility" or "of ignoble blood."

This word "despised" is very commonly understood. It comes from the Greek word *exoutheneo* and also means "contemptible, that which is least esteemed, or that which is considered nothing." God has intentionally opted to use that which is despised and ignoble in this world.

Paul went on: *"and the things which are not, to bring to nothing the things that are."* This is such a great phrase! Paul is saying that not only has God chosen things that are considered "nothing," but He has chosen things that actually are nothing, and He has done it *"to bring to nothing the things that are."* The Greek word translated *"bring to nothing"* is *katargeo* and means "to abolish, destroy, make of no effect, vanish away." What does God want to abolish and make disappear? It is *"the things that are."*

That's strange, isn't it? *"Things that are"* what? Things that are *"wise"* and *"mighty,"* things that are "sophisticated" and "powerful." God not only does not want to use such things, but He wants them to be totally shown up for what they are. His desire is that they be made to totally vanish. Wow!

Verse 29 then gives the resounding motivation for all of this: *"that no flesh should glory in his [God's] presence."* I believe that there is a truth here that most of us have not yet profoundly understood. When, in Romans 13:7, God speaks of giving *"honor to whom honor is due,"* it is not some kind of permission for flesh to *"glory in [God's] presence."* Romans 13:7 and 1 Corinthians 1:29 are not contradictory scriptures — they just need to be contextually understood.

The *"honor"* spoken of in Romans 13 was clearly intended for figures of authority. It does not refer in any way to movie stars, star athletes, famous singers and the like. It was most certainly not for ministers of the Gospel. The word translated "honor" is the Greek word *time* (pronounced tee-may). The primary meaning of this word is "money paid" or "valuables," but it also means "to esteem." We are all advised to "honor" the various branches of civil leadership, but the "esteem" we give them is based on their positions as civil servants and not as ministers of Christ. We ministers of Christ are simply not allowed to steal the glory of the One we represent. If someone wants to be thankful to God for us, that's fine, but if we in any way position ourselves to receive perceived credit for ministry, we violate the spirit of 1 Corinthians 1:29.

The word translated "glory" in this verse is from the Greek word *kauchaomai,* meaning "to wrongfully take credit." The phrase "in His presence" is from the Greek word *enopion* that means "in the face of." God does not deem it acceptable when we allow our faces to be spotlighted when only He is to be spotlighted. This explains why He intentionally chooses vessels that are so inglorious as His favorite vessels of real power.

God cannot work with "glory thieves." This is not because He is insecure or must be patronized or catered to. It is, in fact, God's deep longing to share His glory with us that motivates Him. This is the irony of it all.

God knows, however, that no man who tries to put his own face where only God's face should shine can be trusted with receiving actual glory. This, after all, was the very sin that caused Lucifer to be cast out of Heaven. It is no small thing.

Isaiah recorded Lucifer's fall:

> *How you are fallen from heaven, O Lucifer, son of the morning! How you are cut down to the ground, You who weakened the nations! For you have said in your heart: "I will ascend into heaven, I will exalt my throne*

above the stars of God; I will also sit on the mount of the congregation on the farthest sides of the north; I will ascend above the heights of the clouds, I will be like the Most High." Yet you shall be brought down to Sheol, to the lowest depths of the Pit. Isaiah 14:12-15

Verse 14 reveals Lucifer's desire: *"I will be like the Most High."* The words are deceptive. When "glory robbing" first shows up, it disguises itself as "glory sharing." Lucifer said, *"I will be like ..."* This did not seem to be a direct affront to God, but it clearly was so. The very desire to "share" what is only God's is Luciferian. God insists that we be free from spotlight hunger. Again, this is not because He feels insecure, but rather because He desires to see us free from this core satanic influence in our lives. God's will is that *"no flesh glory in His presence."*

When the serpent deceived Eve in the Garden of Eden, it was with this same subtle temptation. He said, *"... eat ... and you will be like God"* (Genesis 3:5). This is the central error of New Ageism and other Eastern religious thought — that we somehow become divinity ourselves, that we are God or Godlike. This is the core of all satanic deception, and it has, unfortunately, invaded the Church through the pervasiveness of ambition and self-promotion.

This is a grave danger. Lucifer did not fall because of a lack of giftedness or even a lack of calling. He fell because he could not conquer his need to *"ascend."* I fear that many "stars" of the church world are in similar danger today. Their giftedness and calling is undeniable, but these cannot secure for them an eternal position. This is why — by intentional design — God has reserved the greater giftedness and anointing for the foolish and the weak.

Most of those whom God desires to use are yet part of a great sleeping army. They have been deceived into thinking that they can do little for God because of their inadequacies. It is my hope that this book will wake up many who are in that condition. It is time for God's army of weak, small and foolish ones to arise; the Master calls.

In closing this first chapter, let us reread 1 Corinthians 1:27-29, this time in my paraphrase of the original Greek:

But God has intentionally picked that which is considered by this world to be foolish, or even moronic, to totally shame and show up that which is sophisticated and seemingly impressive. And God has, on purpose, chosen the unimpressive, feeble and frail things of this world to totally shame and show up that which is boisterously impressive. And also the ignoble, low-class things of the world and the things that are completely overlooked and despised, God has, by divine intent, chosen; and the things that are not sophisticated, impressive or powerful, to disgrace and humble things that are so. And it's all that no human being would steal the glory that is due only Him.

CHAPTER 2

A MAN OF SORROWS

Who has believed our report? And to whom has the arm of the Lord been revealed? For He shall grow up before Him as a tender plant, and as a root out of dry ground. He has no form of comeliness; and when we see Him, there is no beauty that we should desire Him. He is despised and rejected by men, a man of sorrows and acquainted with grief. And we hid, as it were, our faces from Him; He was despised, and we did not esteem Him.

Isaiah 53:1-3

As we follow this unusual thought of being weak, small and foolish enough to really be used by God, let us re-examine the life of Jesus, our Savior, for He is our supreme example. Did His life follow the guidelines of 1 Corinthians 1:25-29?

Was He or was He not a living demonstration of the foolishness of God confounding the wisdom of men? Would we have been impressed with Him or might we have even overlooked Him? What if He were disturbingly unimpressive? Let us consider these questions as we read Isaiah's description of Him.

Verse 1 begins with a reference to the end of the previous chapter, where Isaiah had spoken of the Messiah as one who would dumbfound kings: *"and kings will shut their mouths because of him"* (Isaiah 52:15, NIV). The first line of this new chapter, *"Who has believed our report?"*, is translated in *The Living Bible* as, *"But, Oh, how few believe it! Who will listen?"*

Verse 2 tells why few would believe. First, the Messiah would come *"as a root out of dry ground."* He would come during a season when very little faith or hope existed. He was not the by-product of revival. He came during the height of the dominance of Greek philosophical thought. Faith was at its lowest ebb, and "critical thought" was at its height.

Besides His coming forth from the *"dry ground,"* there was more. The Messiah would have *"no form or comeliness,"* *"no beauty"* that men should desire Him. This word, "form," in the original Hebrew was *toar* and meant "outline, figure, or appearance." The Hebrew word translated as "comeliness" was *hadar* and meant "magnificence, beauty, or glory." Not only was the Messiah's "figure" not good, but He was not attractive. The fact that He had no *toar* implies that both His height and build were below average. It also implies that His physical appearance (including His face) were less than outstanding.

Just in case we haven't gotten the picture, Isaiah tells us that there was *"no beauty"* in Jesus. This word "beauty" comes from a third Hebrew word for unattractive — *mareh*. The word means "that which you would see if you looked in a mirror." Isaiah was covering all the bases with his description of the Messiah. Jesus would have neither *toar*, *hadar* or *mareh* to make us desire Him.

If we look back at the three original Greek words used in 1 Corinthians 1:26-28 to describe those chosen by the Lord, we see that they fit Jesus as well. *Moros* meant that He not only did not have a look of sophistication, but failed even the look of intelligence. *Aesthenes* meant that He looked a little frail and feeble. And *agenes* meant that He hadn't even appeared to come from respectable genes. Nothing about Jesus' physical appearance or demeanor drew positive attention to Him.

Verse 3 of Isaiah 53 declared, *"He is despised and rejected by men."* I am convinced that this was true of Jesus even before He reached His time of ministry. This word, "despised," is from the Hebrew *bazah* and means "disdained, scorned and thought of as a vile person." The Hebrew word for "rejected" is *chadel*, meaning "an unpopular outcast."

This is not much of a Messianic package so far, is it? If it seems like I'm being redundant, that's just the point. Why are the Scriptures so redundant on this point if not to emphasize an important fact? And because the Scriptures continue to make the point, so must I.

Verse 3 continues: *"A man of sorrows and acquainted with grief. And we hid, as it were, our faces from Him; He was despised, and we did not esteem Him."* An intriguing observation about this verse is the use of the word *"we."* We are all included. "We" were ashamed of Him, and "we" did not esteem Him. This was clearly meant to speak to the Jews who would ardently seek the Messiah in every generation and to forewarn them not to look for an impressive "Messiah package." Rather, the Messiah would be the antithesis of what they might expect. He would not just offend them with His Gospel, but His very physical presence would be offensive as well.

This theme continues in verse 4: *"Yet we esteemed Him stricken."* This word, "stricken," meant "leprous or plagued." The forewarning to those who would earnestly seek the Messiah was that they would be repulsed by the ignobility and ingloriousness of His physical presence.

Verse 10 is a seemingly harsh one: *"Yet it pleased the Lord to bruise Him."* The Hebrew word translated here as "bruise" is the word *daka*, which means "to crumble." Why would the Father be desirous of so weakening His Son? Was it not because *He has chosen the weak things of this world to confound the things that are mighty*? And if God did not destine Jesus, the Head, to come in an impressive human form, what could His desire be for those of us who make up His Body?

Other portions of scripture also tell us about Jesus' weaknesses. The Father used other things besides Jesus' physical deficiencies to "crumble" Him. For one, the Jews, God's people, were repulsed by Jesus. They considered Him to be a bastard. He came from a very insignificant town. His very accent, no doubt, belied His lack of nobility.

Everything about Jesus' early days was intentionally unimpressive, inglorious and unworthy of esteem. If He had been born in an emperor's palace, perhaps He would have stood a better chance of impacting those He came in contact with. But God chose the stable.

Jesus could have grown up in Rome and been trained in sophisticated philosophical debate. Some probably felt that His teachings would have been easier to understand if He had been "properly trained." But God chose Galilee as the early training ground for His Son.

Why did the Messiah grow up working with His hands (as a carpenter) when He would have to minister to people who needed to be intellectually impressed ? Wouldn't academic training have provided Him better tools for ministry? Actually, no, because God has chosen the foolish things of this world to confound the wise.

One of the deceptions that has infected our contemporary Christianity is a half-truth. There is an acceptance of the benefit of small or humble beginnings, but by and large, such beginnings are considered to be only a transition period to greatness and glory. This supposedly gives us the right to self-promotion. Eventually, we are expected to start acting like the king's kids we are. The problem is that we model our conduct on the children of earthly kings. In Matthew 21, Jesus left us a picture of our heavenly King, and that picture does not quite mesh with our accepted concepts:

> *Tell the daughter of Zion,*
> *"Behold your King is coming to you,*
> *Lowly, and sitting on a donkey,*
> *A colt, the foal of a donkey."*   Matthew 21:5

This passage refers to Jesus' triumphal entry into Jerusalem, but I believe it also carries prophetic connotations (I will get to these later). First, however, let us examine the attributes here ascribed to our King. What is the first attribute given to Him?

Jesus is not described here as "majestic," or "imposing," but rather as *lowly*. What does *lowliness* have to do with being a king? With an earthly king, lowliness may indeed be out of place, but lowliness has everything to do with who our King was. This word, "lowliness," is not a misprint or a misrepresentation of facts, and it is not an isolated thought. Here is what our King said of Himself:

> *Take my yoke upon you and learn from Me, for I am gentle and LOWLY*
> *IN HEART, and you will find rest for your souls.*   Matthew 11:29

This is one of the most insightful passages in the Bible. What we often fail to see is that when Jesus humbled Himself, it was not a disguise: He was actually *"lowly in heart."*

Jesus was not just lowly in action. His lowliness came forth from His *lowly ... heart.* The reason God *"resists the proud"* is not that He is in some tug of war with man for power and glory. Our Lord resists the proud by sheer instinct. He *is* humble, and therefore, He cannot even relate in intimacy with those who are not like-*hearted*.

There are ministers representing Christ on Earth who have an impressive record of Kingdom building (in our eyes, at least), yet our lowly Lord cannot necessarily relate to these people. He, being lowly, has a built-in resistance to those who are "highly," even if they seem to be accomplishing much for Him.

There are other scriptural passages that confirm these truths:

> *Many will say to me in that day, Lord, Lord, have we not prophesied in thy name? And in thy name have cast out devils? And in thy name done many wonderful works? And then I will profess unto them, I never knew you: depart from me, ye that work iniquity.*   Matthew 7:22-23, KJV

These verses are not speaking about false religions. This is a warning to Christians. How could those who prophesy, those who cast out devils, and those who have done *many wonderful works* be considered workers of iniquity? Is that not severe? How can such wonderful works ever be considered an act of iniquity? The answer is that if we have misrepresented the heart of the King, our kingdom work is not His. Operating without humility is the evidence of being out of relationship with Him.

As an added note, false humility is worse than overt pride. False humility only disguises various forms of self-promotion.

Returning to Matthew 21, Jesus had spoken to two of His disciples:

> *Go into the village opposite you, and immediately you will find a donkey tied, and a colt with her. Loose them and bring them to Me. And if any-*

one says anything to you, you shall say, "The Lord has need of them," and
immediately he will send them.   Matthew 21:2-3

Our great King could have requested any number of more glorious animals to ride on for His Triumphal Entry into the city of
Jerusalem. Did the disciples just happen upon a donkey and use it
because it was convenient? No, not at all. This was not a matter of
convenience but one of intentional design. Jesus *chose* to use the
donkey.

Jesus' first words to His disciples that day had been, *"Go into the
village opposite you ... ."* It was going to require effort to find this
donkey.

If Jesus had wanted to impress the people, He could have made
His Triumphal Entry into the city on the back of a lion. That would
have seemed more appropriate for a King. If He didn't want to ride
a lion, at least He could have mounted a majestic white stallion.
Surely there was some form of transportation more "kingly" that
He could have chosen. There may have been, but He chose to ride a
donkey.

Triumphal Entry? What Triumphal Entry? A short, feeble-
looking, homely guy riding on the back of a little donkey. That
doesn't seem like much of a Triumphal Entry to me. It seems more
like divine foolishness.

If Jesus had the option of coming into the city in "excellence,"
why would He have not chosen something that made more of an
impression? It is because He has always chosen the weak, the small
and the foolish.

Jesus didn't just request a donkey. He instructed His disciples to
find a tied donkey and to loose it. What that means to us is that it is
not enough just to be a weak, small and foolish package. God cannot
use us until we have been loosed. How do we get loosed? It is by
waking up to the realization that the very things that we feel disqualify us for service are the very things that might make us God's
first choice. He is looking for the weak, the small and the foolish,
and many of us qualify.

Again, why does the Lord seek such servants? It is, He said, *"That no flesh should glory in His presence."* Could a donkey ever steal glory from the Lord? Of course not. So, Jesus chose to enter the city on the back of this inglorious animal:

> *And a very great multitude spread their garments on the road; others cut down branches from the trees and spread them on the road. Then the multitudes who went before and those who followed cried out, saying: "Hosanna to the Son of David!*
> *'Blessed is He who comes in the name of the Lord!'*
> *Hosanna in the highest!"*   Matthew 21:8-9

Notice that no attention whatsoever was being paid to the donkey. The crowd did not chant, "Hosanna to the Lord and to His donkey." A donkey is so inglorious that to consider him in any way as being relevant seems foolish. Still, the donkey *was* relevant in his own way. He was the means that Jesus chose to use to carry Him into the city. What could be more relevant?

Still, the donkey didn't brag. How could he? Picture for a moment the face of your average donkey. These animals look goofy and almost moronic. The sound a donkey makes is often ridiculed, as well, and rightly so: Hee haw; hee haw. Couldn't it just bring forth a respectable neigh? Yet the Lord chose the donkey.

After Jesus chose the donkey and commanded it to be loosed, He explained why. He needed it. My premise (one that I am only now beginning to develop) is that the Triumphal Entry was a prophetic picture, and that the Lord is now preparing to make His final Triumphal Entry. When He does, He will manifest His presence as never before, and He will choose to *need* many donkeys to help Him.

Others are offering the Lord rides, but many of these seem to want a share of His glory. Jesus is coming with power and glory, but His glory will be clearly seen only on those who are willing to keep their heads down and allow Him to be seen over them (as a donkey would). Because *the foolishness of God is wiser than men"* (1 Corinthians 1:25), multitudes will come forth to follow Jesus and to worship Him as they did when He entered the city of Jerusalem that day. But not everyone will receive Him, just as was true on that day. The full, the learned, and the sophisticated of the Church may miss Him again. They won't even be in the right part of town. The multitudes, however, will find Him and worship Him, as they did when He came riding into Jerusalem:

And when He had come into Jerusalem, all the city was moved.

Matthew 21:10

Some may misconstrue the message of this book as being anti-intellectual. That's not the actual point. However, there is an important message on the heart of God. He wants to loose donkeys who have been tied up too long. If that offends intellectuals, I'm sorry. My mission is to loose donkeys, and therefore, I will continue to develop this theme. In the coming chapters, I will use many other scriptures and biblical examples. I will also use personal testimonies — all to drive home this important point to our hearts. The 1 Corinthians 1:25-29 model has always been and will always be the modus operandi for *real* Kingdom advancement.

JESUS' FORERUNNER

In those days John the Baptist came preaching in the wilderness of Judea, and saying, "Repent, for the kingdom of heaven is at hand!" For this is he who was spoken of by the prophet Isaiah, saying:
"The voice of one crying in the wilderness:
'Prepare the way of the LORD;
Make His paths straight.' "
And John himself was clothed in camel's hair, with a leather belt around his waist; and his food was locusts and wild honey. Then Jerusalem, all Judea, and all the region around the Jordan went out to him and were baptized by him in the Jordan, confessing their sins.   Matthew 3:1-6

John the Baptist was the forerunner whom God used to introduce the Savior to the world of his time. There could not have been a more important assignment. Surely, we would think, God would have wanted someone impressive to do this work. Yet He chose John, a man who wandered in the desert dressed in camel's hair, eating strange food and crying out, "Repent."

Most of us might have considered John to be a "nut," but God used him: *"Jerusalem, all Judea, and all the region around the Jordan went out to him."* People were drawn to John in droves. He didn't go looking for them; they came looking for him. People responded to John's message; crowds of them were baptized by him in the Jordan River.

This was no mere ceremony. These people were *"confessing their sins."* What was motivating them? What was drawing them out of the cities to the banks of the Jordan River? What was causing them to be sorry for their sins and be willing to forsake them? This sounds very much like the crowds that later followed Jesus.

We have only begun to understand the power that is available to us when we move aside and let God work through us. This matter of the power of Christ resting upon us is much greater than we have yet to imagine. When His power is upon us, things are accomplished that transcend our natural thinking.

The real anointing is carried in the spirit realm, not in the brain. John spoke out of his spirit, and what he said impacted the spirits of those around him. He didn't worry about working on his communication skills. He didn't do a test run of his message before some lesser crowd. He didn't seek the advice of experts to help him weed out distracting elements from his presentation. And since John was the first preacher of the New Testament era, maybe we should emulate his methods, rather than those of the modern preachers of today.

Real preaching releases the power of the Lord. Silver-tongue orators may draw a crowd, but real preaching is spirit-to-spirit. It is possible to both preach and orate, but to the degree that we lean on our oratorical skills, to that same degree we quench the Spirit. John had the power of God at work in his ministry, for it was a ministry that leaned on the Holy Spirit.

JESUS' DISCIPLES

Although John was chosen to introduce Jesus, the men the Lord chose to be the pillars upon which the entire Church would be built were apparently no less lacking in impressiveness than John. Most of them were fishermen from a notoriously backward part of the country, and at least one of them was a tax collector — the most despised profession of the day.

On the Day of Pentecost, when the Spirit was poured out on the disciples, people who heard them speak were amazed by who they were:

> *Then they were all amazed and marveled , saying one to another, "Look are not all these who speak Galileans? And how is it that we hear, each in our own language in which we are born?"* Acts 2:7-8

Those who witnessed the events of that day were perplexed and asked, *"Whatever could this mean"* (verse 12)? How could ignorant Galileans be speaking many strange languages? It was because God had chosen the foolish things of this world to confound the wise. Jesus wasn't forced to choose fishermen. There were other people available. He wasn't forced to choose a tax collector. He wasn't forced to use Galileans. This was His choice, His preference, and He is still in the business of using the weak and lowly of this world.

In God's sovereignty, He chose our Messiah to come from unimpressive human stock. He also chose the Messiah's forerunner to be humanly unimpressive. Then, finally, the Messiah's disciples, those on whom the whole Church would be built, were another intentionally unimpressive lot. None of them smoothed out their wrinkles or polished up their act. They all remained true to the "package" they were sent in. May the truth of 1 Corinthians 1:25-29 truly sink into our Spirits.

CHAPTER 3

DEMONSTRATION OF THE SPIRIT
AND OF POWER

And I, brethren, when I came to you, did not come with excellence of speech or of wisdom declaring to you the testimony of God. For I determined not to know anything among you except Jesus Christ and Him crucified. I was with you in weakness, in fear, and in much trembling. And my speech and my preaching were not with persuasive words of human wisdom, but in demonstration of the Spirit and of power, that your faith should not be in the wisdom of men but in the power of God.

1 Corinthians 2:1-5

PAUL, AS AN EXAMPLE OF APOSTOLIC FOOLISHNESS

There is a common saying, "A picture is worth a thousand words." I firmly believe that if we could all look at an actual photograph or painting of Paul and see what he looked like, it would save us a thousand words. We are told by some credible, though extra-biblical, sources that Paul was not a physically impressive person. Apparently he was frail-looking, balding and quite bowlegged, and it is possible that he had very bad eyesight. Nor was he averse to saying as much himself, as he clearly did in this passage.

Verse 1 begins with Paul acknowledging a lack of giftedness in his preaching. Today, we would take that as proof that a person was not called of God to preach. At the very least, we would insist that the preacher "polish" his communication skills before he proceeded. A large part of most seminary preparation is dedicated to the assurance that 1 Corinthians 2:1 will *not* be the personal testimony of those who graduate. This, again, exposes our tendency to deception in this area.

We all agree that God uses an inferior or imperfect product if He has to, but we are sure that He would *prefer* excellence if He had a choice. But we are so wrong in this matter.

When we feel this way, we are motivated by the same feelings that affected some of the disciples. They were constantly trying to "upgrade" Jesus so that He would represent a more worthy Messianic package. The tragic error is that to the degree we "upgrade" the original designed package, to that same degree we lose the power released through that package. Jesus *had* to be born *in a manger* and *of a virgin*. It was a distasteful "package," but it was not an optional one. God did not *prefer* a palace and an experienced mother. Jesus came the way God *chose* Him to come.

In verse 3, Paul said, *"I was with you in weakness, in fear, and in much trembling."* Why had the Damascus-road experience not cured him of this problem? This word translated "weakness" here is the same root word used in 1 Corinthians 1:27, where it says: *"God has chosen the weak."* We notice again the use of the word *chosen*. This is God's choice.

The word translated "fear" here is the original Greek *phobos,* and the word translated "trembling" is *tromos,* which means "to quake with fear." In English, we speak of a *phobia,* meaning an associative fear (as opposed to a general fear). This means that a fear is triggered by a certain situation. What Paul is saying here is that the very act of preaching would trigger in him a response that produced not just *"trembling,"* but *"much trembling."* The service that he was dramatically arrested by God to perform was the very service for which he appeared to be totally unqualified. If only Paul could have attended a good seminary, some might think, he would have learned how to conquer this enemy of his ministry and, thus, he would have enhanced his gift. God chose to use him just as he was.

There was more to Paul's weakness. In verse 4, he said, *"And my speech and my preaching were not with persuasive words of human wisdom."* In case we hadn't understood what he was saying in verse 1,

Paul wanted to make it clear. The word I find interesting in this phrase is "persuasive." In the original Greek, this word was *peithos*, which meant "to convince, pacify or conciliate through reason or argument." Many Christians and virtually all preachers seem on a mission to be *peithos*. This is what seminaries, Bible schools and discipling programs are all about. Paul said, however, that this was not how he chose to come to the Corinthians.

In Chapter 2, we saw that this was also true of Jesus. Some would have considered it "too bad" that both Jesus and Paul were not nearly as "enlightened" as we are today. We have learned how to incorporate *peithos* into our Christianity. Of course, we do seem to have lost the power. Could there be a connection?

With all his lack, there was something that Paul did have: *"But in demonstration of the Spirit and of power."* These nine simple words comprise one of the most significant and powerful phrases in the entire Bible.

What is this word, "demonstration"? The original Greek word was *apodeixis* and meant "to exhibit, manifest or show off." The word translated "Spirit" was *pneuma*, and it meant "breath or wind." *Pneuma* can speak of the Holy Spirit Himself or of breath or wind created by Him. This word "power" is from *dunamis*. *Dunamis* means "miraculous power" or the miracle itself that is evidenced by force and violence. This is not a passive "power." It helps us to understand it when we remember that we get our word "dynamite" from *dunamis*.

It amazes me that some "good Christians" who seem to love the Lord cannot accept manifestations of God's power unless they are specifically mentioned in the Bible. But demonstrations of the power of God made up the only type of church meeting that Paul knew anything about. His meetings were a stage where the Holy Spirit "showed off" the power of God. In Paul's meetings, I am sure, people shook, fell, cried and laughed. Emotions were touched, and bodies were healed. The power in those meetings was visible and evident, and it was important to Paul that it happen in each of his meetings because he had nothing else to fall back on. He certainly couldn't rely just on his words.

I am convinced that the only reason Paul did not explain what all these "manifestations" consisted of is that such manifestations were so common in his day that there was no need to explain them. In each meeting, he experienced a demonstration of *pneuma* and of *dunamis*. If there had been no presence and no power of God, then Paul would have had no ministry.

Today, we have ministry with no power and no presence, and it is the result of replacing the need for the demonstration of God's presence and power with persuasive wisdom. Crowds followed those who possessed persuasive wisdom in Paul's time, and they still do today. But this was not the ministry of Jesus Christ or of His true servants.

What Paul said in verse 5 of this second chapter of First Corinthians is "huge." He declared: *"That your faith should not be in the wisdom of men but in the power of God."* Even the very first word of this verse is insightful. The word is *"that,"* and this "that" shows that there was purpose to all that preceded it. There was a conscious intent on God's part for Paul being the way he was.

This was not just a curious aspect of Paul's character or style. Coming in power and not in mere persuasiveness was considered to be a prerequisite for the true Gospel, and it still is today. Faith that is built on our intellect is not faith at all. Real faith must be based on a demonstration of the power of God.

It's not just that it requires faith to see the miraculous. We must be exposed to the miraculous in order to grow in faith. Faith shrinks where reason and intellect are deified, and faith grows where demonstrations of the Spirit and power are evidenced. This understanding constitutes *true wisdom*, as opposed to human wisdom.

Human wisdom is not just that which proceeds from non-Christians. Human wisdom is that which proceeds from the intellects of all men, whatever their status in life.

Paul showed the Corinthians that there was a wisdom to be had: *"But we speak the wisdom of God in a mystery, the hidden wisdom which God ordained before the ages for our glory"* (1 Corinthians 2:7). That's the wisdom we seek.

Demonstration of the Spirit and of Power

Paul went on to describe the operation of such wisdom:

> *But God has revealed them to us through His Spirit. For the Spirit searches all things, yes, the deep things of God. For what man knows the things of a man except the spirit of the man which is in him? Even so no one knows the things of God except the Spirit of God. Now we have received, not the spirit of the world, but the Spirit who is from God, that we might know the things that have been freely given to us by God. These things we also speak, not in words which man's wisdom teaches but which the Holy Spirit teaches, comparing spiritual things with spiritual. But the natural man does not receive the things of the Spirit of God, for they are foolishness to him; nor can he know them, because they are spiritually discerned.*
>
> 1 Corinthians 2:10-14

One of the greatest areas of confusion among Christians is knowing what value to place on the written Word of God. Some groups are guilty of not valuing it nearly enough, but many others are guilty of making the Bible into a god. I call it "bibliolatry." Verse 10 does not say that God reveals His wisdom through the Bible or even through the study of the Bible. His Wisdom is revealed through His Spirit.

Verse 11 goes on to tell us that only God's Spirit can reveal Christ to us. Those who are guilty of "bibliolatry" allow the Bible to usurp the rightful seat of the Holy Spirit. The Bible is the instruction manual to the Vehicle, but the Vehicle is the Holy Spirit. The instruction manual is worthless apart from the Vehicle. The manual itself reveals this:

> *Who also hath made us able ministers of the new testament: not of the letter, but of the spirit: for the letter killeth, but the spirit giveth life.*
>
> 2 Corinthians 3:6, KJV

We are to be ministers, not of the written Word, but of what the Holy Spirit has breathed into that written Word. If our intellect ministers the letter of the Word, it is not just vain. It actually has power to destroy.

Many of us have the smug notion that if people just knew enough of the Bible, we would all live in some sort of spiritual bliss. The truth is that the greatest divisions in Christian circles have always been perpetrated by those who are the most knowledgeable concerning the Bible. We presently have over 10,000 different Christian denominations. Each of them was started by someone who supposedly knew the Bible well. The longer the Bible has been available to us, the more divisions have sprouted. The Bible has been turned into a rubber element. It has been stretched to say and support almost every imaginable belief. It is a proven instrument of destruction — when it is not breathed upon by the Spirit.

Aside from the thousands of existing Christian denominations, there are many other religions that are based on the Bible. Jehovah's Witnesses, Mormons and even some Moslems have their traditions rooted in this book. Some of the most confused people I know are virtual memory banks of the written Word. The written Word of God, without the illumination of the Holy Spirit, kills. It is not even neutral.

We have been taught that the greatest deed the Lord did for us was to leave us His Word. "Yes, He ascended back to Heaven," we are told, "but He didn't leave us alone. He left us the Word." This is usually the cue for us to utter shouts of praise. But when Jesus gave His final instructions to the disciples who would then lay the foundations for the Church, He told them to *"wait for the Promise of the Father"* (Acts 1:4). *"The promise of the Father"* was not the Word, it was the Holy Spirit.

Jesus could have made things much easier for us by sharing just who had apostolic authority to write under inspiration. That would have saved three hundred years of serious dispute and many more years of lesser dispute over this issue. In His final words to His disciples, however, Jesus didn't even address the issue of the value of the written Word. Instead, He informed His disciples that the significant thing He was leaving was His Spirit:

But you shall receive power when the Holy Spirit has come upon you; and

you shall be witnesses to Me in Jerusalem, and in all Judea and Samaria,
and to the end of the earth.   Acts 1: 8

If the most important thing for the men Jesus had handpicked and invested in for more than three years was to interact with the Holy Spirit, how could it be any different for us today? We act like Jesus' primary concern was that we have the Bible so that we can be proper Christians. His final concern for His disciples, however, was that they have an encounter with the Holy Spirit, so that they might receive *dunamis* to properly represent Him. Without being empowered by the Holy Spirit, these men had no hope of extending the Kingdom of God.

Writing to Timothy, Paul warned that we should avoid a *"form of godliness"* that denies the *"power"*:

Having a form of godliness but denying its power. And from such people
turn away!   2 Timothy 3:5

This word, "form," is from the Greek word *morphosis* and means "appearance" or "formula." Sadly, most of us get our formulas from the letter of the word.

Please, don't misunderstand what I am saying here. Every single word of the Bible is precious when "breathed upon" by the Holy Spirit, but when the Spirit has not breathed into those words, they become tools of deception and destruction.

Remember that the devil attempted to use scripture as a tool to deceive Jesus Himself. We find an important example of this in Matthew 4:

Then Jesus was led up by the Spirit into the wilderness to be tempted by
the devil.   Matthew 4:1

Jesus was led by the Holy Spirit into what follows, and in the next verses we can clearly see both the letter and the spirit of the Word at work:

31

Now when the tempter came to Him, he said, "If You are the Son of God, command that these stones become bread."
But He answered and said, "It is written, 'Man shall not live by bread alone, but by every word that proceeds from the mouth of God.' "
Then the devil took Him up into the holy city, set Him on the pinnacle of the temple, and said to Him, "If You are the Son of God, throw Yourself down. For it is written: 'He shall give His angels charge concerning you,' and 'In their hands they shall bear you up, lest you dash your foot against a stone.' "
Jesus said to him, "It is written again, 'You shall not tempt the Lord your God.' "
Again, the devil took Him up on an exceedingly high mountain, and showed Him all the kingdoms of the world and their glory. And he said to Him, "All these things I will give You if You will fall down and worship me."
Then Jesus said to him, "Away with you, Satan! For it is written, 'You shall worship the Lord your God, and Him only you shall serve.' "
Then the devil left Him, and behold, angels came and ministered to Him.
Matthew 4:3-11

There is power in the written Word when it is spoken under the inspiration of the Holy Spirit. Jesus used the Scriptures to defeat Satan, and His use of them was very effective. But isn't it revealing that when the devil goes for "high-level" deception, he too uses the Scriptures? This was not a one-time aberration. If the written Word were so powerful in itself, how could it allow itself to be used by Satan? Satan was quoting out of Psalm 91.

Psalm 91 is a powerful passage full of powerful promises, and many of us cling to those promises. The parts of it that Satan quoted in that moment seemed to be applicable to Jesus' situation, but what would have happened if He had obeyed? If Jesus had relied in that moment on a surface knowledge of the Bible, the results would have been tragic. Thank God that He relied on the Holy Spirit, and the Spirit turned the written Word into a mighty weapon for Him. This illumination of the Holy Spirit, not some memorized verse, became the key to Jesus' victory that day.

What a scene that was! The King of the Universe and the villain of the Universe were both using the same book against each other. And the same thing still happens today. Study does not, of itself, make the Scriptures anointed. It is the illumination by the Holy Spirit that makes them anointed. This point cannot be made too much nor too strongly. Reason-and-intellect-driven Bible study proves nothing. The Holy Spirit teaches us as we seek His guidance. He releases wisdom into our spirits that can then feed our minds.

This reestablishes the truth Paul was making in 1 Corinthians 2:11, *"No one knows the things of God except the Spirit of God."* It is impossible for us to be out of fellowship with the Holy Spirit and learn the things of God — even if we were to memorize the entire Bible. This is not my idea. The Bible itself says it, warning of those *"who exchanged the truth of God for a lie, and worshipped and served the creature rather than the Creator"* (Romans 1:25).

This word, "creature," refers to that which is created. The Bible is an awesome creation of God, but when we substitute relationship with the written Word for relationship with the Spirit, we become idolatrous. We can live through interaction with the Holy Spirit (even separated from the Bible), but the Bible without the Holy Spirit is not only lifeless, it is dangerous.

Through the centuries, millions of innocent people have been killed to the rallying cry of men and women quoting the Scriptures. During the Crusades, the Inquisition and in many wars, the Bible was used as a license to kill. This is because *"the letter killeth."*

In 1 Corinthians 2:13, Paul said, *"These things we also speak, not in words which man's wisdom teaches."* Each of us should ponder those words and allow them to sink deeply into our hearts. If we are unable to speak with words that are somehow different than that which *"man's wisdom teaches,"* it should trouble us, particularly those of us who are preachers or teachers.

Today, we extend serious training on how to speak to those who would be ministers. We teach aspiring ministers "effective communication skills," but do those communication skills rely on the work of the Holy Spirit? Are we teaching our young men and women to speak out of their heads rather than out of their spirits? Are we communicating to them well enough the fact that it is the work of the Holy Spirit to convict sinners? Or do we expect our evangelists to apply mental pressure to move people to Christ?

The Kingdom of God advances Spirit to spirit, not intellect to intellect, and that's what the rest of verse 13 goes on to say: *"but which the Holy Spirit teaches, comparing spiritual things with spiritual."*

In verse 14, Paul declared: *"But the natural man receives not the things of the Spirit of God, for they are foolishness to him; nor can he know them, because they are spiritually discerned."* This is another very important statement. It does not imply only that non-Christians are incapable of receiving the things of the Spirit of God. The Greek word here translated "natural man" is *psuche* and speaks of basic humanity. It means "breath" or "spirit," but not the immortal breath or spirit. We could say it in this way: "Human brain waves do not receive the things of the Spirit of God." Why is that? Because the things of God strike our human brain as being foolish, or, as the original Greek word, *moria,* denotes, "absurd" and "silly."

When we receive Jesus, we do not get an automatic upgrade of our minds. They must be renewed by the Spirit. Marching around Jericho must have seemed as foolish to the Israelites who did it as it did to those who watched it from the confines of Jericho. The Israelites did it because of the *hidden wisdom* that descended from above.

The fact that Jesus expected one boy's lunch to feed a multitude was as absurd to His disciples as it was to everyone else who was present that day, but they obeyed because of the hidden wisdom they received. What I am trying to show is that Christians are no more prone to think with God's logic than are non-Christians. The reason for this fact is given in verse 14: *"Nor can he know them."* In other words, our natural minds have no ability to "get on line" with God's logic. It can't happen because the things of God must be *"spiritually discerned."*

This means that we must investigate under the inspiration of the Holy Spirit. He must become our Teacher. We cannot simply suppose that because we are saved, the Holy Spirit is our Teacher. Yes,

He wants to teach us, and He is available to teach us. But if we don't bow our minds to His seemingly mind-boggling wisdom, then we are not really learning the things *"of the Spirit of God."* We may be obtaining persuasive information, but it will be marked by power-lessness, and according to Paul (in 1 Corinthians 2:5), that would be an improper foundation for our faith.

From a priority standpoint, we must understand the proper relationship between the Word, our brains and the Holy Spirit. Both the Word and our brains must bow to the Holy Spirit. The Holy Spirit is not to bow before either our brains or the Word.

Many are frightened by this kind of talk and call it "experiential theology." They are afraid that we are removing all the objectivity of the written Word. But again, I remind the reader of the thousands of denominations that exist based on the supposed clarity of the written Word of God. Predestination or free-choice; congregational leadership, presbyterian leadership or episcopalian leadership; fasting is good or fasting is bad; community is good or community is bad; works are essential or works are not needed ... the list goes on and on. Every conceivable viewpoint can seemingly be supported by scripture.

The Word that we must come to know best is Jesus Himself (see 1 John 1). Yes, it is of great value to study the Bible, but with the stipulation that we have a real and interactive relationship with the Holy Spirit. Without that, studying the Bible becomes counterproductive.

Conversely, a living relationship with the Holy Spirit will automatically increase your hunger for the written Word of God, because the Word, when inspired by the Holy Spirit, is the revelation of Jesus Christ. It is not a manual to defend your doctrinal position. It is the disclosing of who Jesus really is, of all that He has done, and of all that He will yet do.

We cannot skip the relationship part and go directly to the understanding of the Word anymore than we could have a baby without first having a sexual union. We cannot have an understanding of God's Word apart from union with His Holy Spirit. He must become our Helper and our Teacher, for our Savior sent Him for that purpose:

These things I have spoken to you while being present with you. But the Helper, the Holy Spirit, whom the Father will send in My name, He will teach you all things, and bring to your remembrance all things that I have said to you.   John 14:25-26

In these verses, we find two key works that the Holy Spirit will do for us. He will bring things to our remembrance, and some have limited Him to this — but there is more. We have the promise: *"He will teach you all things."* The Spirit reminds, but He also teaches:

However, when He, the Spirit of truth, has come, He will guide you into all truth; for He will not speak on His own authority, but whatever He hears He will speak; AND HE WILL TELL YOU THINGS TO COME.   John 16:13

What does the Spirit do? He guides us into all truth, and He tell us about things to come. Must all the things the Holy Spirit tells us about the future be already written in the Bible? Of course not. The Holy Spirit has permission to tell us of things to come, even if they are not written in the Bible. The Bible itself gives Him this permission.

A friend of mine, who is a pastor in Honduras, was there when Hurricane Mitch struck that nation. Before the exact trajectory of the storm had even been determined, the Holy Spirit spoke to him and told him to take all his money and all the money of the church and buy food because the storm would surely hit their small town. When he met with the other leaders of the church and told them what God had said, there were some tense moments. What if he was wrong? What if they bought tons of food and then the storm passed them by? All their money would be gone, and they would have a mountain of perishable food on their hands.

Think about it. Try to put yourself in that man's position. Did the Bible say that Mitch would strike that particular town and leave devastation in its wake? What evidence did he have that this would really happen? The answer is that he had none. All he knew was that the Holy Spirit had told him to prepare.

In the end, those leaders trusted their pastor, and the food was bought. Hurricane Mitch hit Honduras with devastating force, pounding much of the nation for the next seven days. All power was lost. Roads were washed away, and the little community where my friend lived was isolated for the next forty days. Because he had heard from God, however, he was able not only to save himself and his church; a thousand people were fed for thirty desperate days.

On day three of the storm, the Holy Spirit told the pastor something else. He was to go and warn some of his members who lived in a specific part of town to get out of their houses. It was in the early morning hours when he got this word, but he went quickly and told his people what God had said. They listened to him and vacated their houses. Within hours, a nearby river had overflowed its banks. It opened up a new course and carried away ten of the homes of the believers in that area. Other homes were carried away too, and the people were still in them. The believers in that town were spared because they hearkened to the words of the Holy Spirit. The promise is true: *"He will tell you things to come."*

If the Holy Spirit has no extra-biblical freedom, we are all in trouble. How could we know whom to marry? How could we know what job to pursue? How would we answer dozens of other important questions in life. The Holy Spirit is available for *all truth.*

The idea of following the Holy Spirit in this way frightens some because they are sure that many will be deceived into thinking they are hearing the voice of the Lord when, in reality, they are not. And it does happen — just as people are deceived in their interpretations of the Bible. Both methods present their risks, but we must use the plan Jesus recommended. That "plan" is the Holy Spirit as our Teacher and Guide. He is the source to the hidden wisdom Paul spoke of.

Paul's identification with weakness and simplicity is firmly established in his writings. He spoke of it over and over again in an attempt to expose the sophistication of men for what it was.

The tenth chapter of 2 Corinthians is a very important one in this regard. In this chapter, Paul seems to be defending himself from charges of being *too* unimpressive:

I plead with you — yes, I, Paul — and I plead gently, as Christ himself would do. Yet some of you are saying, "Paul's letters are bold enough when he is far away, but when he gets here he will be afraid to raise his voice!" I hope I won't need to show you when I come how harsh and rough I can be. I don't want to carry out my present plans against some of you who seem to think my deeds and words are merely those of an ordinary man. It is true I am an ordinary, weak human being, but I don't use human plans and methods to win my battles. I use God's mighty weapons, not those made by men, to knock down the devil's strongholds. These weapons can break down every proud argument against God and every wall that can be built to keep men from finding him. With these weapons I can capture rebels and bring them back to God, and change them into men whose hearts' desire is obedience to Christ. I will use these weapons against every rebel who remains after I have first used them on you yourselves, and you surrender to Christ.

The trouble with you is that you look at me and I seem weak and power-less, but you don't look beneath the surface. Yet if anyone can claim the power and authority of Christ, I certainly can. I may seem to be boasting more than I should about my authority over you — authority to help you, not to hurt you — but I shall make good every claim. I say this so you will not think I am just blustering when I scold you in my letters.

"Don't bother about his letters," some say. "He sounds big, but it's all noise. When he gets here you will see that there is nothing great about him, and you have never heard a worse preacher!"

This time my personal presence is going to be just as rough on you as my letters are!

Oh, don't worry, I wouldn't dare say that I am as wonderful as these other men who tell you how good they are! Their trouble is that they are only comparing themselves with each other, and measuring themselves against their own little ideas. What stupidity!

But we will not boast of authority we do not have. Our goal is to measure up to God's plan for us, and this plan includes our working there with you. 2 Corinthians 10:1-13, TLB

In verse 1, Paul began with the words, *"Now I, Paul, myself am pleading with you by the meekness and gentleness of Christ — who in presence am lowly among you, but being absent am bold toward you."* There are several important things to notice in this verse. First, Paul was pleading with the Corinthian believers that they remember *"the meekness and gentleness of Christ."* He admitted that his own presence was *"lowly."* This word means "offensively unimpressive," and that's precisely what Paul was. He was so naturally unimpressive that he was asking them not to confuse his weakness with a lack of spiritual authority. The entire passage is so straightforward that I encourage those who are hungry for a greater understanding of it to read it over one more time.

We must not allow Paul's experience to have been in vain. In many ways, the church has not been sufficiently impacted by this and other similar passages. How did leading a church become associated with smooth talk and smooth image, when neither Jesus nor Paul would have agreed with it? How very far have we fallen!

Are there perhaps Pauls living among us today whom we fail to recognize because of their apparent weaknesses? If Paul came today, would we receive him? I fear not. While thousands of us read and quote his words every Sunday, I am afraid that we might have found his actual person to be offensive, and we might have considered his message to be irrelevant. Would some of us be offended by Jesus if He came back and appeared to us in bodily form? I'm afraid that many of us would.

This is an important issue. If we are programmed to reject those who are most like Christ, what can our future be? In Paul's day, men said of him, *"When he gets here you will see that there is nothing great about him, and you have never heard a worse preacher!"* What determines for us whether or not a person is worth listening to? Are we sometimes rejecting Christ by rejecting those He sends?

In verse 3, Paul said, *"It is true that I am an ordinary, weak human being, but I don't use human plans and methods to win my battles."* He went on to explain (in verse 4), *"I use God's mighty weapons."* If this is a foreign concept to you, don't let it remain that way. Nothing could be more important.

In verse 5, Paul insisted: *"These weapons can break down every proud argument against God and every wall that can be built to keep man from finding him."* Paul had mighty weapons that destroyed the walls of man's reasoning. In the original Greek, this word translated "proud argument" was *logismos.* It is *logismos* that keeps men from finding God. The word literally means "computing" and "reasoning." As a point of reference, a similar word *logios* means "eloquence" or "orator." Not only did Paul have no "eloquence," but he recognized the exalting of "eloquence" as a wall that separates God from man. Paul was determined to use his mighty spiritual weapons to tear down that wall and all walls associated with the exaltation of reason.

GOD'S POWER IS DEMONSTRATED IN CHIMBOTE, PERU

Later in the book, I will be exploring more of my own experiences with God's willingness to use the weak, small, and foolish, but here I would like to insert just one example to bring home the point Paul was making about the needed demonstration of God's power.

Although I was born in Peru to missionary parents and raised in that country, I first preached there in 1996. It was my first trip back to that country in some fifteen years. One night on that trip I preached in a Baptist church in Chimbote. God had spoken to me to go there. The pastor there was open to the things of the Spirit, and he welcomed me.

I had been touched in a special way by the Holy Spirit through the "Toronto Blessing" (as it has come to be called). Until that happened, I had had no intention of ever doing "the missionary thing" again. I had "been there" and "done that." But after God touched my heart in Toronto, I became a different person. Now, I was in Peru preaching the Gospel.

I had a small team with me, but I was to be the principle speaker. At this time in my life, public speaking was not at all a gift. I was unaccustomed to public speaking in any language, but especially Spanish, which complicated my difficulty. Because of this, I had taken time to write out my entire message ahead of time. So, as I stood before the Baptists that night in Chimbote, I read my message.

The message was about God being "on the move" in these last days and how He is releasing His power and doing things in a moment's time that used to take what seemed like forever. I told the people that the Holy Spirit was going to touch them physically that night and that I was sure they, too, would never be the same again. They would never forget this night, I assured them, because the Holy Spirit was about to reveal Himself in their midst as never before.

As I was reading this message, it seemed like "good stuff" to me, but when I looked up to see how it was being received, I was not encouraged at all. For one thing, I was suddenly aware of the silence in the place. I wasn't hearing even a weak, "amen." Then I realized that nobody was even nodding. In fact, no one even seemed to be smiling. The entire congregation seemed to be frighteningly cold. In this way, it slowly dawned on me that the people had no idea what I was talking about. The Holy Spirit *physically* touching them? What could that mean?

Strangely, I was not discouraged by all this. Despite the cold reception to my message, my faith seemed to soar. Suddenly, I was saying things that I had not written down, things that were coming to my spirit. I told the people that God knew that their church was made up of a high percentage of women, and that it was okay. He was going to use that fact. I told them that God was raising them up as intercessors and that He would do great things through them. Soon, I told them, their wayfaring sons would be returning home to the church, and it would become a training center for young people to be sent all over the country.

I was stirred by all this and expected them to be stirred, too, but you could still hear a pin drop in the church. I hadn't seemed to raise their faith level at all.

As I finished my message, I told the people that it was time for an encounter with the Holy Spirit. We were scheduled to leave town on a bus at 11:30 that night, so I threw all caution to the wind. The pastor had told me that I could minister freely, so now I took full advantage of his graciousness.

I asked the young men who were standing by the back doors to close them so that no one would go out. Then I asked that all the pews be moved to one side so that we would have more open space up front. I instructed the people to line up in rows with five or six feet in between each row. Before long, I had all the somewhat-shocked congregation in place to receive something from God.

About this time, the pastor sent his keyboardist to the platform to play music for this ministry time, but something told me that he should not play. These people were somewhat skeptical of the things of the Spirit. I didn't want anyone to say later that we had manipulated them in any way. "We're going to do this without music," I announced.

I asked all the people to hold their hands out so that they could receive from the Holy Spirit. They obeyed. "Now," I said, "I'm going to ask the Holy Spirit to come and minister to you. What I want you to do is just wait, nothing else."

I prayed a very simple prayer. "Holy Spirit, come." Then we waited for two or three minutes. Nothing happened.

I had determined that we would not begin to lay hands on the people until they knew for themselves that the Holy Spirit was present. When nothing seemed to be happening, I was tempted to go ahead and start laying hands on them. But I didn't. If God wasn't going to come with His power, I might as well just walk out the door and forget it. Somehow, though, I knew that He would.

"Let's just keep waiting," I encouraged the people. And we did.

Then suddenly, a man on the front row fell backward onto the concrete floor. He was unhurt. The man standing beside him went down in the same way. All of a sudden, the power of the Holy Spirit was clearly present.

Loud wailing broke out among some of the people, and others experienced uncontrollable laughter. Many of the people began to shake violently. I looked around to see how the pastor was responding to all this and found that he was on the floor himself, and he was also shaking violently.

All of a sudden, it was evident to me what Paul meant in 2 Corinthians 2:4, when he said that he had come not in words, but in *"demonstration of the Spirit and power."* Now I had a visible demonstration of what he meant.

Whether Paul had those very same demonstrations of the Spirit's power or not is unimportant. I knew that these were signs that the Holy Spirit was at work. We had invited His presence, and He had made Himself known.

"Were these possibly demon manifestations?" What did Jesus say about that?

> *Or what man is there among you who, if his son asks for bread, will give him a stone? Or if he asks for a fish, will he give him a serpent? If you then, being evil, know how to give good gifts to your children, how much more will your Father who is heaven give good things to those who ask Him!*
> Matthew 7:9-11

With these words, Jesus showed that if we ask our heavenly Father for the Holy Spirit, what we receive is the Holy Spirit, not some counterfeit. The reason I bother to present this verse at all is that some are so blinded by unbelief that they attribute anything they are not familiar with or have not previously experienced to Satan. We must be careful when we attribute holy things to the evil one. There is a line that we may cross that is dangerous.

When we have a demonstration of the Holy Spirit and power, there is always good fruit. That night in Chimbote, many people were healed of their diseases. For example, the pastor's wife had suffered three recent miscarriages and was still childless. One of our team members, a twenty-year-old man who knew absolutely nothing about her problem, walked up to her while she was weeping and shaking and said to her what the Holy Spirit had dropped into his spirit: "God is healing your womb." He later told me that he hadn't even realized what he was saying. Ten months later, the pastor's wife gave birth to a healthy little girl.

About a year later, I made another trip to Peru. This time I was preaching in Lima. When the pastor from Chimbote heard that I was in the capital, he took the six-hour bus ride to come and see me. He had called first and told me over the phone that he had many things to tell me. He also wanted me to pray for him again.

When we were able to speak in person in Lima, he proceeded to tell me more about what had happened in the year since we were with him that one night. "Everything you prophesied has come to pass," he began. This was the first time I had thought of what I had said that night as being prophecy. I had just been repeating what I was hearing in my spirit, but now God had brought it to pass.

The church in Chimbote had gone through a transformation, beginning that night we were there. The pastor related to me many of the individual testimonies of people being healed from sickness and depression. And, just as I had said, God had begun to send them many young men, and they now had a Bible institute where they were training these young men to go out and minister.

The church had conducted some special tent meetings a few weeks after we left, and all the same manifestations of the Holy Spirit that we experienced there in the church had taken place in the tent. In one meeting, the pastor related, the presence of the Holy Spirit had come with such force that the tent shook violently. At first, people began running out, thinking that it was an earthquake. Then, they realized that it was the Holy Spirit. There were many testimonies of healings and deliverances at those meetings as well.

Recently, the pastor and his wife (and their two-year-old daughter) visited us here in the United States for several weeks. Somehow we had developed a supernatural bond. I had not been back to Chimbote, and on the occasion we had been there, I hadn't even been able to spend a full day in the city. All of this had come about through a single meeting. When the Holy Spirit manifests Himself, it makes all the difference.

During the time the pastor and his wife were here with us, they continued to testify of the ongoing move of God in their church that began that night. They are now sending out missionaries around the country. They recently had a special day of evangelism, and two hundred and forty-six sinners came to the Lord. They continue to see signs and wonders, healings and deliverances, and they continue to desire more of God.

The pastor's wife asked me if I had noticed that first night in Chimbote how closed to the Spirit the people of the church had been. I told her I had. She said that she had been one of the "resistors" that night but that the Lord had totally broken down the walls of resistance in her. He had done it through His mighty weapons (see 2 Corinthians 10:4).

I am keenly aware that a book has a very wide audience and that I may well be addressing people on all sides of this issue of signs and wonders. Surely, some of you who read this are also "resistors," like that pastor's wife. Some of you have a deep hunger for the moving of the Spirit, but for various reasons, you feel that you are not qualified. It is time to free yourselves from the shackles of men's wisdom and move into the power that is available for you today.

Paul went on, in the next chapter of 2 Corinthians, to share his great concern:

> But I fear, lest somehow, as the serpent deceived Eve by his craftiness, so your minds may be corrupted from the simplicity that is in Christ.
>
> 2 Corinthians 11:3

How was it that the serpent deceived Eve? First, he asked her, "Has God said?" (Genesis 3:1). The enemy still tries to corrupt our minds in that same way. He asks, "Has God said ... that these signs will follow those who believe (Mark 16:17)? Has He really said ... that healing is for today? Has He really said that you would be endued with power when the Holy Spirit has come upon you (see Acts 1:8)?" In this way, through *craftiness*, he has robbed the Church of nearly all of its supernatural inheritance. This word "craftiness" in the original Greek is *panourgia*, and it means "sophistry." Our enemy has us eating from *"the tree of the knowledge of good and evil"* instead of from *"the Tree of Life."*

Good and evil, pro and con, the whole process of reasoning and dispute is what Satan has offered us instead of simply life. Sadly, we have wholeheartedly partaken of it, and it has brought death. Simple obedience, not connected to the mind of reason, produces life. That offends those who are in idolatry to reason, but it is nevertheless the truth.

Several years ago, I was invited by a pastor friend of mine in Chicago to hold some meetings in his church. It was a young church that had never had more than thirty-five members, and that included the children. I was asking the Lord what I should share with them during their Sunday morning meeting, when He reminded me of the great Chicago fire. It had been started by Mrs. O'Leary's cow kicking over a lamp. I felt that the Lord was showing me that I could serve as a cow in that church to start the fire. The Lord would be the Wind that carried the fire.

I bought a lamp in Atlanta and took it with me to the meetings in Chicago. I told the people what God had showed me and told them that I intended to kick over that lamp (unlit), expecting the Holy Spirit to take care of the rest. You can imagine how intelligent I looked doing all that. It wasn't very sophisticated, but I felt God was going to honor it. You see, I really believe that God has chosen the *"foolish things ... to confound the things that are wise."*

At the end of my message, I kicked over the lamp. We didn't see any sparks, and nothing else phenomenal seemed to happen, but within two weeks, the attendance in the church had risen to a hundred and ten, and there seemed no way to explain it. Since then, the church has suffered the ups and downs common to all congregations, but from the day of that prophetic act forward, it has been a very different congregation.

The people of that church are now taking trips to the nations. Most recently, they took a team of about twenty for two weeks of meetings in the Dominican Republic, and they came back with many great testimonies. Was it all because of me? No way! But somehow a "foolish" act of obedience was used to expedite some things that the Lord had been wanting to do.

This leaves me with a question for some of you who are reading this, those of you who feel you can't preach, can't sing, and have no gifts. Could you at least kick over a lantern? If so, then God can use you, too.

The church in Chicago left that lamp overturned on their platform for many months ... until they eventually had to seek a larger building to move to. They knew what it symbolized and recognized what the Lord was using.

But sometimes the foolish things we do will be understood by no one but God. If what we do has been ordained by Him, it will have powerful results. God does not need our "brains" or our "muscles." He only needs our obedience.

We cannot finish our discussion of Paul and his example of weakness without looking at his teachings in 2 Corinthians 12. This is the chapter where Paul revealed the often-discussed *"thorn in the flesh."* Was it bad eyesight? Was it lust? Was it a demon? I've heard all those views espoused. However, I want to look beyond these speculations and try to see what Paul was really saying:

> *Concerning this thing I pleaded with the Lord three times that it might depart from me. And He said to me, "My grace is sufficient for you, for My strength is made perfect in weakness." Therefore most gladly I will rather boast in my infirmities, that the power of Christ may rest upon me. Therefore I take pleasure in infirmities, in reproaches, in needs, in persecutions, in distresses, for Christ's sake. For when I am weak, then I am strong."*
>
> 2 Corinthians 12:8-10

An experience that I had in the Dominican Republic finally brought this truth home to me. We had been in several days of great meetings there, and one night, after a particularly powerful meeting, we ate some bad fish. What we suffered from it was far worse than the food poisoning we at first thought we had. We were infected by a neurotoxin known as the red tide poisoning. I had never been so sick in my life. I vomited and had diarrhea until I rapidly began to dehydrate and had to be given electrolytes. The pastor's wife nearly died from it and had to be hospitalized for several days.

Finally, the worst seemed to be behind us, but we were wrong. After the initial food-poisoning symptoms, the infection then changed gears and began to affect us in other ways. Those who are interested may look up the term "red tide poisoning" to see for yourself what all is involved. This infection is often deadly and stays in the body, on average, for up to a year or two. I was in bed every day for about a month, until God instantly healed me one day.

During the days I was still in the Dominican Republic, it was a particular trial. We thought we had just suffered from food poisoning and that we were now over it. The next day was Sunday and our last day on the island, and I decided that I could still preach. I was too weak to stand during the worship, but I was anointed enough by the Lord to give a short message and lead a ministry time for the church of about nine hundred members.

Finally, it was time to leave, and I began weakly making my way down the aisle toward the back of the church. As I was doing this, many of the Dominicans came up to give me a last hug and to say how much they appreciated what God had done through all the team members on this trip. Then, an interesting thing happened, something that had never happened to me to this degree before (and it has never been repeated to this degree since). As the people hugged me, they would "fall out" on the floor, and I was having to catch them, one by one, after hugging them.

What was so amazing to me about this was that I was feeling very bad physically. I was so sick that I couldn't feel the presence of the Lord in any way myself. What I felt was weakness, but as Paul said, *"The power of Christ was resting upon me"* (2 Corinthians 12:9). As the people would hug me, they would break into tears and then fall and lie there shaking for a long while. The Holy Spirit seemed to be stronger when I was weaker. It was in that moment that I understood for the first time how Paul could boast in his infirmities.

What credit could I take for the power flowing through me? None! It would have been foolish to try. I had nothing to do with it. The more of me that was out of the way, the more the Spirit could do.

The final phrase of 2 Corinthians 12:10, I believe, is often misunderstood and even misquoted. It doesn't say, "For when I feel weak, I should try to act strong." It says, *"For when I am weak, then I am strong."* I was strong in spirit, while being weak in the flesh. The two went together. I wasn't trying to do a psyche job on myself. It just happened.

We must not take lightly the lessons of Paul's life. He was not just a gung-ho Christian through whom the Lord did great things, even though he himself was unimpressive. That's the wrong message. When we say that God has used us, "even though ... ," we are suggesting that He prefers better stock. The truth is that He *chooses* the foolish. When He uses the foolish, He receives all the glory.

When Paul had his conversion experience on the road to Damascus, he was chosen by God for service. What happened that day was divine intervention from Heaven. A light that left Paul blind for three days shone from Heaven, and he was thrown to the ground. What was God looking for in a man? Paul was not a good speaker; he was bowlegged; he was a murderer whom the church would find hard to trust for a long time to come. He was apparently divorced; he had bad eyesight; he was seemingly a horrible candidate ... and yet ... and yet ... and yet has there ever been a person whom God went more out of His way to recruit than Saul of Tarsus?

Are we getting it yet? God has *chosen* the weak things of this world. He has *chosen* the despised. He has *chosen* the foolish things — and not because He has no other choice. This is God's *first choice.* If you are "impressive" and God is using you, then be shocked. If you will take off some of the polish, maybe He'll use you even more. When you risk being foolish, you position yourself to make a greater impact in the spirit realm.

Chapter 4

Arise, Anoint Him, for This Is the One!

And Samuel said to Jesse, "Are all the young men here?"
Then he said, "There remains yet the youngest, and there he is, keeping
the sheep."
And Samuel said to Jesse, "Send and bring him. For we will not sit down
till he comes here."
So he sent and brought him in. Now he was ruddy, with bright eyes, and
good-looking. And the Lord said, "Arise, anoint him; for this is the one!"

1 Samuel 16:11-12

As we have seen, all the principle New Testament characters were notoriously inglorious in their presentation — when judged in the natural — and the very same is true of the men and women of the Old Testament whom God chose to use. This makes us to know that choosing an inglorious package has always been the Lord's chosen method of operation. Surely this is an important truth, one that should be given more consideration.

Some of us may know this truth in our heads, but it is time that it penetrates our spirits. When it does, it will change forever the way we live and behave. That is why I continue to make this point over and over again. This truth must be *"made flesh"* and allowed to free us to new possibilities in the Lord.

If David is not the best-known of all Old Testament figures, he is, at the very least, near the top of that list. Most of us probably know his story well. In light of the truth we are discussing, however, let us review several aspects of David's life.

First, we remember that David was the replacement king who took power only after the Lord had rejected His original choice, King Saul. Saul had been chosen of the Lord, but when God chose him and placed him in office, Saul had been a humble man. When Samuel went to find him to anoint him as king over Israel, he could not be found because he was hiding among the baggage (see 1 Samuel 10:32).

When Saul became proud, Samuel was again sent to him, this time to inform him that God had rejected him:

> *So Samuel said, "When you were little in your own eyes, were you not head of the tribes of Israel? And did not the Lord anoint you king over Israel?"*
> 1 Samuel 15: 17

God had originally chosen Saul because he was *"little in [his] own eyes."* Something had happened to him, and he was no longer *"little in [his] own eyes"*? It had been said of Saul:

> *And he had a son whose name was Saul, a choice and handsome young man. There was not a more handsome person than he among the children of Israel. From his shoulders upward he was taller than any of the people.*
> 1 Samuel 9:2

Saul was the best-looking man around, and he was the tallest man around. When he received the power to rule over the nation, it seems to have gone to his head. He could not bear it, and it ruined him, and Samuel was sent to "un-anoint" him.

Saul's story is a most important "case history," and each of us must learn from it. Saul's life shows us clearly why God chooses to release His great glory through what we might call "handicapped vessels." The tendency of all men is toward pride, and if there is no daily reminder in our lives that "it is not about me," then deception can begin to set in. Indeed, our tendency toward pride is the most dangerous foe we all must face. It is impossible for human glory and heavenly glory to coexist. God will not share His glory with another.

Saul reigned only a few years under God's anointing. His entire reign lasted forty years, but the final thirty-seven years of it were with the stamp of the Lord's rejection upon him. Sadly, we must say that this is also the case with many formerly-anointed men and women of God. They had God's anointing, when they were *"little in [their] own eyes."* Now, they may still be "king," they may still be doing what it was they were doing before, but the glory of the Lord has departed from them. His *"gifts and callings are without repentance"* (Romans 11:29, KJV), but a person may still be stamped "rejected by the Lord" while yet operating in those *"gifts and callings."* This was certainly true in Saul's life. He still had his position before the people, but he had lost his position before God.

It was then that God sent Samuel to anoint a new king (although it would be years before this fact was widely known by the people and before David would actually take office).

When Samuel arrived at the house of Jesse, he began to examine the man's sons:

> *So it was, when they came, that he looked at Eliab and said, "Surely the Lord's anointed is before Him."*
> *But the Lord said to Samuel, "Do not look at his appearance or at the height of his stature, because I have refused him. For the Lord does not see as man sees; for man looks at the outward appearance, but the Lord looks at the heart."*
> *So Jesse called Abinadab, and made him pass before Samuel. And he said, "Neither has the Lord chosen this one." Then Jesse made Shammah pass by. And he said, "Neither has the Lord chosen this one." Thus Jesse made seven of his sons pass before Samuel. And Samuel said to Jesse, "The Lord has not chosen these."*
> *And Samuel said to Jesse, "Are all the young men here?"*
> *Then he said, "There remains yet the youngest, and there he is keeping the sheep."*
> *And Samuel said to Jesse, "Send and bring him. For we will not sit down till he comes here."*
> *So he sent and brought him in. Now he was ruddy, with bright eyes, and good-looking. And the Lord said, "Arise, anoint him; for this is the one!"*

Then Samuel took the horn of oil and anointed him in the midst of his brothers; and the Spirit of the Lord came upon David from that day forward. So Samuel arose and went to Ramah.   1 Samuel 16:6-13

The next verse begins with the terrifying words: *"But the Spirit of the Lord departed from Saul"* (1 Samuel 16:14). It was time for another man to be raised up to take the helm.

We can assume from Samuel's reaction at seeing Jesse's son Eliab that he still held in his mind the physical appearance of Saul. Because Eliab was so physically impressive, Samuel assumed that he was surely the one God had chosen. The Lord had to specifically tell Samuel, *"Do not look at his appearance or at the height of his stature."* Until that moment, Samuel may not have realized that Saul's physical beauty and height were not what caused God to consider him. He only looks at the heart: *"For the Lord does not see as man sees."*

For some reason, David was not brought in with his other brothers to meet the man of God. Jesse was aware that one of his sons was about to be anointed king, but in his mind, there was no way that it could be David. This is interesting because David was said to be very good-looking. Perhaps that was only Samuel's observation. Maybe David's "ruddy" complexion mentioned in the Scriptures (usually meaning either redheaded or of reddish skin, or both) just didn't strike Jesse as something that was "kingly."

Saul had set a high standard for what a king should look like. He was, perhaps, dark-haired and dark-eyed and that became the "kingly model," rather like the "cookie-cutter" preachers being turned today. Something about David caused his own father to believe that he could not possibly be the one for the job. He didn't fit the mold.

It was not Jesse who volunteered the information that there was yet another son; Samuel had to ask. Why would this father not have made sure that his youngest son was present at this most-important of occasions? We can't say for sure. Why did the other brothers not insist that David have a chance? We don't know. What we do know is that neither David's father nor his seven other brothers could imagine that he would be chosen by God for anything of importance.

It is very possible that the perception your family has of you has kept you back as well. Have you been unable to overcome the unkind thoughts and words of those around you? What if God is waiting to anoint you, and you have allowed others to disqualify you? What if your family members are wrong about you? It is time to loose yourself from any restriction placed upon you by others. You may be just the donkey the Lord is looking for.

David had a cross to bear, and that cross was the rejection of his family. But God has chosen the *"despised."* Sometimes we can be despised because we are obviously inglorious, but sometimes people just look for something to despise in us.

In the well-known story of David and Goliath, David was coming to bring food to his brothers, but he was stirred to see the situation in which they and the other Israeli soldiers found themselves. They were being harassed by a great giant of a man.

David knew immediately that Goliath could be defeated, and he didn't mind saying so. His brothers, however, were not very happy with his outspokenness on this matter:

> But when David's oldest brother, Eliab, heard David talking like that, he was angry. "What are you doing around here, anyway?" he demanded. "What about the sheep you're supposed to be taking care of? I know what a cocky brat you are; you just want to see the battle!"
>
> 1 Samuel 17:28, TLB

What a terrible statement! Could there have been anyone more clueless about who David really was than this brother at that moment? David was just moments away from killing the giant who had all of Israel trembling, and what did his oldest brother do? He called David *"a cocky brat."* This was the same brother who so impressed Samuel, the prophet, and the same brother who then watched as Samuel anointed David to be the next king over all Israel. How could Eliab now accuse David of being *"cocky"*?

Nothing that we know about David ever suggests pride or cockiness, and the Lord Himself called David *"a man after [My] own heart."* David's psalms reveal him as a broken and contrite man. He had sins, but none of them seem to be related to the accusation his brother made that day. As I thought about this enigma, the Lord showed me that envy often sees boldness as cockiness. It is possible that every humble-yet-bold servant of the Lord has been accused of pride at some point.

David seemed to take this all in stride, and we must learn to do the same. His first hurdle was to go through this "family thing," to suffer the petty charges made by his loved ones, and he passed with flying colors.

David eventually got King Saul's attention, but that encounter did not go very smoothly either:

> *When it was finally realized what David meant, someone told King Saul, and the king sent for him.*
> *"Don't worry about a thing," David told him. "I'll take care of this Philistine!"*
> *"Don't be ridiculous!" Saul replied. "How can a kid like you fight with a man like him? You are only a boy and he has been in the army since he was a boy!"* 1 Samuel 17:31-33, TLB

David could not seem to escape the *"cocky brat"* label. Now, it was the King, and he was saying that David was being *"ridiculous."* He called him *"a kid."* This must have been hard for David to bear. After all, he had already been anointed to replace this king, he was about to bring a great victory that would save the entire country, and this man was calling him *"a kid."*

David, however, was not oversensitive. This is something that every David-want-to-be must remember. David wept bitterly when Saul died despite the treatment he had received from him. Although David was here being belittled for his youth, he wasn't about to let that stop him. He responded to the king very politely, but very positively and boldly:

Arise, Anoint Him, for This Is the One!

But David persisted. "When I am taking care of my father's sheep," he said, "and a lion or a bear comes and grabs a lamb from the flock, I go after it with a club and take the lamb from its mouth. If it turns on me I catch it by the jaw and club it to death. I have done this to both lions and bears, and I'll do it to this heathen Philistine too, for he has defied the armies of the living God!"
1 Samuel 17:34-36, TLB

These acts of which David spoke were supernatural. How could such a small and young man kill bears and lions with his bare hands and a small club? That had to be a miracle. So David's confidence was not just braggadocio. He had grown accustomed to defeating big enemies under the power of God's anointing. The only problem was that others didn't know about it yet. Soon, however, they would.

I have heard it preached that the lion and the bear prepared David for Goliath. Although that is probably true, I don't believe that it was easier to kill a lion or a bear than it was to kill Goliath. It must have been infinitely more difficult to grab a lion by the jaw and kill him than it was to kill an eight-foot-tall man. I think David also knew this, and that was precisely his point. He considered what lay ahead to be much easier than what he had already done, and that's why he was so eager to go after the giant.

Did David have a preconceived strategy for killing Goliath? I don't think so. He just knew that if he stepped into the supernatural, it would happen, and it would happen easily.

God has His modern-day Davids. Late one night, when we were on yet another ministry trip to the Dominican Republic, an unusual thing happened. Our team members were being driven home. Scott, one of our men, was in a van with twelve other people, when they blew out a tire in a very bad part of town. There was no service station around and no phones, and they also discovered that they had no jack. It was clearly a bad situation.

Surveying the situation, Scott decided that he could lift the rear of the van so that the tire could be changed. He told the driver that if he would take off the bad tire and put on the spare, he would hold the van up. Scott then proceeded to hold up the van at about waist height while this process took place.

Thinking about it later, everyone was amazed. You see, Scott is only about five-eight or five-nine, and although he is strong, he is not that strong. Still, he said that the van hadn't even seemed heavy to him.

That van wasn't a small vehicle. It held thirteen people. What Scott did was clearly supernatural. He could not have done that on his own. He was anointed for the task.

Scott is not a preacher or a singer, and he almost never gets "pulpit time." But he doesn't allow that to stop him from being anointed for special tasks. God uses him in amazing ways. Our God is looking for more of these modern-day Davids.

The David of the Bible knew how to move in supernatural power when he was called upon. Eventually, King Saul gave him a chance to show what he could do against the giant. There was only one stipulation: He was to wear Saul's armor. This shows that Saul did not really believe what David was saying about defeating the lion and the bear. If he had believed him, he would have known that David didn't need armor.

I believe there was another issue at play in this situation. We remember that Saul was a head taller than anyone else in Israel, and he must have been considered the logical choice to take on Goliath. (Saul was probably at least six and a half feet tall.) If David were to succeed, he would be showing Saul up for the coward he was. If the men of Israel's army saw *"a kid,"* and a short one at that, leading the charge against the enemy, it would be embarrassing for the king. It seems to me that Saul wanted David to use his armor for two reasons. One, maybe the men would think that it was actually Saul who was taking on Goliath (his armor was surely very recognizable). And two, maybe the armor would make David look taller and more mature and have some psychological effect on the giant.

Whatever the case, Saul's plan didn't work. He was so much larger than David that the lad could barely move about with the king's armor in place. In the end, David refused to wear it, for it would only weigh him down. When you are a David, you cannot wear Saul's armor. New wine requires new wineskins.

Arise, Anoint Him, for This Is the One!

Tradition is the killer of the anointing. Just because a certain methodology has been used to kill so-called Philistines in the past doesn't mean it will work for that purpose today. We can see that Philistines have a tendency to get bigger, and old, outdated methods may no longer take them out. A David's anointing and a Saul's methodology will not mix. Let us learn from David.

David was not done with being disrespected. First, it was his family that despised and belittled him, then it was his king, and now it was the enemy. Goliath was very irritated by David. He was sure that the lad was "in way over his head." Clearly, it was Goliath who had no idea who he was up against.

> *Goliath walked out towards David with his shield bearer ahead of him, sneering in contempt at this nice little red-cheeked boy! "Am I a dog," he roared at David, "that you come at me with a stick?" And he cursed David by the names of his gods. "Come over here and I'll give your flesh to the birds and the wild animals," Goliath yelled.*
> *David shouted in reply, "You come to me with a sword and a spear, but I come to you in the name of the Lord of the armies of heaven and of Israel — the very God whom you have defied. Today the Lord will conquer you and I will kill you and cut off your head; and then I will give the dead bodies of your men to the birds and wild animals, and the whole world will know that there is a God in Israel! And Israel will learn that the Lord does not depend on weapons to fulfill his plans — He works without regard to human means! He will give you to us!"*

> 1 Samuel 17:41-47, TLB

Goliath sneered in contempt, cursed David, and then proceeded to tell the lad how he was going to die. You may have a giant in your life that does the same thing: ridicules you, curses you and tells you how he'll eventually bring you down. But David was wise. He knew that Goliath had no authority to say these things, so he paid no attention to them. Instead, he shouted right back at the enemy, and he made a bold proclamation. This *"cocky brat,"* this *"ridiculous*

... kid" told Goliath, *"I will kill you and cut off your head,"* and then he proceeded to follow through with his proclamation.

This chapter of the Bible has been beloved for centuries. It is inspiring. But this teaching is more than just inspiring; it is also prophetic. In the midst of this last-day outpouring that God is sending upon His sons and daughters, we are destined to do great exploits. (See Daniel 11:32.) There will be many Goliaths, and they will not fail to try to intimidate us. To their surprise, however, the Lord will release previously-unknown champions among us. He is even now preparing us for battle.

These "champions" may not look like champions to us at all. They may come out of total obscurity. But, suddenly, there they will be, viewing the front lines, recognizing how easily victory can come, and carrying out their God-given battle plans.

The world will surely consider that these people are "in over their heads," but that fact will only glorify God all the more as great victory comes. The battle is not ours, but the Lord's. When giants come against God and His people, they are the ones "in over their heads." Great authority is given to common men when they act in the name of the Lord and for His cause. You may be one of God's champions of the end-time. Prepare yourself accordingly.

We all know the ending of the story of little David and big Goliath. David ran out to meet the giant and killed him with a stone from his sling. That was not accidental. David wanted to kill Goliath with the smallest thing he could find, and that happened to be a little stone. This made his point. Then, after that point was made, he took Goliath's own sword and cut off the giant's head. It was a totally anti-climactic duel, for God has chosen the weak things of the world to put to shame the things that are mighty. This has always been His plan, and it will always be His plan.

CHAPTER 5

WHO AM I THAT I SHOULD GO?

But Moses said to God, "Who am I that I should go to Pharaoh, and that I should bring the children of Israel out of Egypt?"　　　Exodus 3:11

Moses might very easily qualify as "Man of the Old Testament." He probably saw more of God's glory than any other figure in the Scriptures. He experienced so much of the glory that his face glowed and had to be covered. The supernatural took place through Moses on a continuing basis. The Red Sea parted for him. The ten commandments were given to him supernaturally. Water came from a rock to give his people drink. And that was just the beginning. Every day there was some new miracle in his life.

Even Moses' death was glorious. He was in full health when he went up the mountain that day, and God took him into His presence in that condition. No wonder then that when Hollywood decided to do a movie about Moses' life, Charlton Heston was chosen to portray him (and he did present an impressive figure). If we read the real story of Moses carefully, however, we find that the man was a far less impressive personality than we might have imagined.

For eighty years, Moses remained ignorant of the greatness God had planted within him. Then, one day, the Lord appeared to him in a burning bush and called him into the ministry. He told Moses that he would be used to deliver Israel out of the hands of the Egyptians. For most of us, a voice coming from a burning bush would have been enough to convince us that what God was saying was true, but this was not the case with Moses:

But Moses said to God, "Who am I that I should go to Pharaoh, and that
I should bring the children of Israel out of Egypt?"   Exodus 3:11

Moses was saying, "Lord, I'm not the man for the job." He was also afraid that no one would believe him if he did speak for the Lord:

Then Moses answered and said, "But suppose they will not believe me or
listen to my voice; suppose they say, 'The Lord has not appeared to you.' "
                                                         Exodus 4:1

Because Moses was not at all convinced that he was the best man for this job or that anyone would pay attention to his words, the Lord had to show him several signs. He caused Moses' rod to change into a serpent and then back again. He had Moses place his hand inside his robe, and the hand became leprous. When he did it again, it was returned to normal. These were powerful signs, but Moses was still not very confident. He still felt very ill-equipped. In part, it seems that he had reason to feel that way:

Then Moses said to the Lord, "O my Lord, I am not eloquent, neither
before nor since You have spoken to Your servant; but I am slow of speech
and slow of tongue."   Exodus 4:10

For some reason, Moses was *"slow of speech,"* and it seems to indicate that he had an actual speech impediment. This could have been something as simple as a lisp, a stutter or an inability to roll his R's, or it could have been something much more serious. Whatever it was, it caused Moses to think that he was not qualified — even after he had seen several supernatural signs.

The Lord had the answer for Moses:

I will be with your mouth.   Exodus 4:12

Moses still objected:

Who Am I That I Should Go?

Lord, please! Send someone else.   Exodus 4:13, TLB

Why did God insist on choosing someone so "wimpy"? Because, as we have seen, He delights in using the unqualified of this world to reveal His glory. The fact that Moses was still resisting His offer eventually angered God:

> *So the anger of the Lord was kindled against Moses, and He said: "Is not Aaron the Levite your brother? I know that he can speak well. And look, he is also coming out to meet you. When he sees you, he will be glad in his heart. Now you shall speak to him and put the words in his mouth. And I will be with your mouth and with his mouth, and I will teach you what you shall do. So he shall be your spokesman to the people. And he himself shall be as a mouth for you, and you shall be to him as God. And you shall take this rod in your hand, with which you shall do the signs."*
>
> Exodus 4:14-17

What a shame! Apparently Moses had such low self-esteem that he could not believe that a God who could speak out of a burning bush was powerful enough to help him speak. Many of us limit the Lord in this same way. *Sure He made the universe,* we think, *but there's just no way He can use ME.* We think our smallness can limit His greatness.

Moses may have lost another significant sign by angering the Lord. Originally, the Lord had said to him, *"I'll be with your mouth."* Now, He adjusted that promise and made Aaron the mouthpiece for Moses.

Country music star Mel Tillis has difficulty speaking because of a stuttering problem. A person hearing him being interviewed would never believe that he could sing like a bird when he's on stage. But he does. Moses' situation must have been similar.

It seems that the Lord was not promising to heal Moses' speech difficulty, but He was promising to anoint him to speak whenever he was "on stage." Many are waiting for God to heal them of their "limp" before allowing Him to use them. Many don't realize that

God is not going to remove the limp as a prerequisite to service. Not only that, but if we artificially have that "limp" removed, we cease to be the vessel of first choice through which He releases His glory. To embrace a limp is to embrace humility. To embrace a weakness is to embrace His right to take the glory. So whatever your "limp" is, embrace it. He wants to use us not just *despite* our limp, but *because of* our limp.

Now, don't misunderstand me. By "limp," I'm not referring to sin or a character flaw in our lives. Let's be clear on this: We must get rid of sin, get rid of pride and get rid of self-sufficiency. God *"resists the proud"* (1 Peter 5:5), so He obviously will not choose that which He is resisting.

Of Moses, it was said:

> *Now the man Moses was very meek, above all the men which were upon the face of the earth.*   Numbers 12:3, KJV

Other versions of the Bible confirm that Moses was the humblest and most gentle man on planet Earth. The original Greek word translated here as "meek" is *anayv* and could easily be translated as, "one having a very depressed view of self."

If we were God, we might have chosen Aaron rather than his brother. If Aaron had to do the speaking anyway, why not just give him the signs and wonders and let him do the job? Could anything be more important than effective communication? Oh, how very far our ways are from God's ways! Far too many of us are deceived in this regard. The Church as a whole seems to have made a conscious decision to never again be laughed at by the world, and we are constantly trying to put our best foot forward. All the while, God is desiring to demonstrate His power through our weakness.

Obviously, there must be a balance in this regard. I am not saying that being uneducated and unglamorous is, in any way, synonymous with being anointed. Ignorance, in itself, does not bring any glory to God. We must say, however, that there has been an overcorrection in this area in recent years. In our desire to present a better face to the world, we have moved more toward professional-ism and away from dependence upon the Holy Spirit. This is dangerous.

The days of the "backwoods" preacher are clearly behind us. We have gained esteem for our ability to be found on the cutting edge of education and technology. But in the process, have we not lost the power of the Gospel? Is there not a direct relationship between the two?

There is nothing wrong with using technology to advance the Kingdom. Let's do it more. What is wrong is our tendency to *lean* on our technologies. This is an important principle that we must learn and teach: to the degree we lean on or trust in technology, that is the degree to which we restrict the Holy Spirit.

This may be the very reason that God did not choose Aaron. Aaron might have depended on someone or something other than God. God purposely chose the least self-sufficient person He could find to perform this most important task. And that person hap-pened to be Moses.

Moses was the meekest man in the whole world, and that is why he saw God's glory manifested so greatly. This is no coincidence! It is not recorded that God spoke face-to-face with any other man, but He did with Moses (see Numbers 12:8). These are the lessons we must learn. If not, we will be constantly offended in the days to come by those who carry great glory. It will baffle our minds and seriously upset us that God would use such people.

"How could God do that?" we might be asking. And if we can't understand how He could use them in this way, we might be prone to consider the signs and wonders they do to be false. We won't have any other way to explain it. Many will still claim to be lovers of God and defenders of His truth, but in reality, they will be strangers to His presence and His glory. Envy will run wild in the ranks of such people, and it will become the silent assassin of many good Christians.

To the degree you find these thoughts irritating as you read this, to that same degree your hollowness will one day be exposed. To the degree you are rejoicing over what you read, to that same degree you may prepare yourself to become a major recipient of the outpouring of these latter days.

Why God Used Jeremiah

We know very little about the personal background of many of the Old Testament prophets. We do know that some of them were asked to do very peculiar things. Hosea, for instance, had to marry a prostitute, and Isaiah was commanded to walk naked backwards for three years (read it in Isaiah 20:2-3 if you don't believe me). It has never been possible to be one of God's prophets without doing some fairly foolish acts in the process of fulfilling His purposes.

Fortunately, we have some background information on Jeremiah and his initial calling, and we can learn from it. Jeremiah was minding his own business one day when the word of the Lord suddenly came to him. He responded with doubts, but God reassured him that he would not be alone in the days ahead. The power of the Almighty would enable him to perform his assigned task:

> *"Before I formed you in the womb I knew you;*
> *Before you were born I sanctified you;*
> *And I ordained you a prophet to the nations,"*

> *Then said I:*
> *"Ah, Lord God!*
> *Behold, I cannot speak, for I am a youth."*

> *But the Lord said to me:*
> *"Do not say 'I am a youth,'*
> *For you shall go to all to whom I send you,*
> *And whatever I command you, you shall speak.*
> *Do not be afraid of their faces,*
> *For I am with you to deliver you," says the Lord.*

Who Am I That I Should Go?

Then the Lord put forth His hand and touched my mouth, and the Lord said to me:
"Behold, I have put My words in your mouth.
See, I have this day set you over the nations and over the kingdoms,
To root out and to pull down,
To destroy and to throw down,
To build and to plant."
Jeremiah 1:5-10

The amazing thing is that Jeremiah was not seeking a prophetic ministry. He had not asked God to make him a man who would change nations. He obviously did not see himself in the same way the Lord did. Suddenly, however, the Lord was there with him and was telling him that he was ordained to be a prophet to the nations.

Jeremiah's response to all of this was understandable: "Lord, You must be kidding, I am young, and I can't even speak." But the Lord told Jeremiah not to disqualify himself in this way. If Jeremiah would be willing to obey this call from God, He would do the rest.

Although Jeremiah was not seeking any special authority, God was clearly releasing it upon him. This had to be a scary experience for such a young man. This, too, will happen often in the days ahead. If you are personally ambitious, God will pass you by, but if God can trust your heart, He will commission you to change nations. In fact, you can get started today. He has said:

Ask of Me, and I will give You
The nations for Your inheritance,
And the ends of the earth for Your possession.
Psalm 2:8

Many of you already have authority and favor in this area, and the Lord is saying to you, "Go for it." If you harbor self-ambition or self-promotion, this encouragement is not for you, for you will dry up on the vine. However, if you are weak, small and foolish enough, He is ready to raise up some of you as Jeremiahs for your generation.

Chapter 6

The Lord Is With You, Mighty Man!

Now the angel of the Lord came and sat under the terebinth tree which was in Ophrah, which belonged to Joash the Abiezrite, while his son Gideon threshed wheat in the winepress, in order to hide it from the Midianites.

Judges 6:11

Gideon is a very well-known Bible figure, and there is much to learn from his life. Most of us have always envisioned him as a very brave warrior who just needed his faith stimulated. This is not the picture the Scriptures paint of him:

When we find Gideon, he is at the bottom of a pit normally used to press grapes. There, at the bottom of that pit, he was threshing his wheat. He was hiding in the pit for fear of the Midianites. Gideon, it seems, had become rather paranoid. Then something totally unexpected happened:

And the Angel of the Lord appeared to him, and said to him, "The Lord is with you, you mighty man of valor!" Judges 6:12

What an amazing statement to make to a man who was hiding in a pit! This angel could have visited Gideon at any other moment, but he chose this particular moment for his visitation. This is in keeping with the pattern we have seen developing throughout the Bible. Some of us have received the most powerful prophecies concerning God's call on our lives when we were in our deepest pit. This has caused us to sometimes wonder about the sanity of the person used as the prophetic voice. Gideon had his doubts too:

And Gideon said to Him, "O my lord, if the Lord is with us, why then has all this happened to us? And where are all His miracles which our fathers told us about, saying, 'Did not the Lord bring us up from Egypt?' But now the Lord has forsaken us and delivered us into the hands of the Midianites."

Judges 6:13

Gideon opened his mouth, and out poured disappointment. Why was that? First, it is important to realize that Gideon did not recognize this messenger as an angel from the Lord. When he called the angel "lord," he was using the Hebrew word *adoni* (not *Adonai*, "Lord"). *Adoni* is equivalent to our word "sir." When Gideon said, *"If the Lord is with us...,"* he *was* referring to God, and the word he used was *Yehovah*, "the self-Existent One." So Gideon, at first, did not know that the person speaking to him was speaking on God's behalf. This same thing happens to many of us today.

Gideon's response is not all that unusual. We are all prone to take advantage of such an opening to let our disappointment come pouring out. "If God is with us, why are we going through so many problems? If God is with us, where are all His miracles?" Most of us have asked these same questions. God may have been great in the past, but Gideon wasn't seeing much of His greatness at the moment.

The Lord answered Gideon with amazing patience and understanding:

Then the Lord turned to him and said, "Go in this might of yours, and you shall save Israel from the hand of the Midianites. Have I not sent you?"

Judges 6:14

Almost as if He hadn't heard a word of Gideon's protest, God repeated His promise and this time made it even stronger. As Gideon was struggling with his first prophecy, he received another one. It was ridiculous enough for him to be called a *"mighty man of valor"* when he was hiding shamelessly in that dark place, but now he was told that he would save the entire nation. This must have seemed *beyond* ridiculous to him.

The Lord Is With You, Mighty Man!

This prophetic word, however, was beginning a process deep inside the young man Gideon. I know how that feels. Some years ago, John Paul Jackson, a prophetic voice, spoke a word that began a similar process deep within me. At a conference, he had my wife and me stand up, and he began to tell us that the very thing I had said I would never do was the thing I would soon find myself doing.

I had made several strong statements at various points in my life, among them was that I would never be a pastor (my dad was one) and that I would never go back to the mission field. Because I had been born and raised in Peru as a "missionary kid," I felt that I had already experienced that life and it that wasn't all it was hyped up to be. I was willing to serve the Lord in some other capacity, but I felt sure that it would not be in these areas.

The prophetic word was detailed and covered many areas, but one of the specific things it brought forth was a calling to the pastoral ministry. God was igniting a special spark within me. After I received that prophetic word, my insides were weak from the impartation of the truth, and I felt drained for the next three days. During those days, the word began to take hold in me. This is what was happening to Gideon:

> So he said to Him, "O my Lord, how can I save Israel? Indeed my clan is the weakest in Manasseh, and I am the least in my father's house."
>
> Judges 6:15

> My family is the poorest in the whole tribe of Mannaseh , and I am the least thought of in the entire family. TLB

I know that something was happening because Gideon suddenly stopped addressing the angel as *adoni* and began calling him *Adonai*. *Adoni* was always used with man, and *Adonai* was always used with God. Gideon now knew that he was in the presence of at least a man of God.

Still, Gideon had serious limitations. He was from the *"poorest"* family, and he was the *"least thought of in the entire family."* That's pretty bad. Again, we see God's method of choosing men and

71

women. He chooses the base, the weak, the foolish, the despised —
that no flesh should glory. Are you perhaps *"the least thought of in your
family"*? If so, then you may be a prime candidate for God's service.

There must have been something in Gideon that caused his
friends and family members to consider him *"the least thought of."*
It's not a very impressive title, is it? When I get to Heaven, I want to
meet Gideon and see what he looks like. I visualize him as being
very short and frail with eyes that bug out, seemingly reflecting
fear. Something about him left everyone around him certain that he
would never amount to much. But God saw Gideon in a totally different light:

> *And the Lord said to him, "Surely I will be with you, and you shall defeat
> the Midianites as one man."*   Judges 6:16

Suddenly, *"the Angel of the Lord"* revealed His true identity. He
was no other than the Lord Himself. He assured Gideon that He
would be with him.

Gideon asked for a sign and proposed that the Lord allow him to
prepare them a special meal. The Lord accepted this invitation and
waited while a goat was prepared. Once the meal was ready,
Gideon was given some special instructions:

> *The Angel of God said to him, "Take the meat and the unleavened bread
> and lay them on this rock, and pour out the broth." And he did so. Then
> the Angel of the Lord put out the end of the staff that was in His hand,
> and touched the meat and the unleavened bread; and fire rose out of the
> rock and consumed the meat and the unleavened bread. And the Angel of
> the Lord departed out of his sight.*
> *Now Gideon perceived that He was the Angel of the Lord. So Gideon said,
> "Alas, O Lord God! For I have seen the Angel of the Lord face to face."*
>   Judges 6:20-22

Gideon fixed the food and set it on a rock. The Angel touched the
meat and bread with his staff, and immediately fire came out of the

rock and vaporized everything. Then the Angel vanished from in front of Gideon. It was only then that Gideon fully realized that he had been speaking with the Lord. He had seen two impressive signs: fire had come out of a rock, and the Lord, who had been there a moment before, had now vanished.

For most of us, that would have been more than enough. We could now have believed that the Lord would back us in whatever He was saying for us to do. But not "wimpy" Gideon. He still needed to be convinced.

The Lord went ahead and gave Gideon his first directive: "Now that you know you're the anointed man of God who will liberate an entire nation, go and tear down the altar of Baal that your father built, and build Me an altar instead" (see verse 25). Gideon did what the Lord commanded ... but only by night:

> *So Gideon took ten men from among his servants and did as the Lord had said to him. But because he feared his father's household and the men of the city too much to do it by day, he did it by night.* Judges 6:27

This *"mighty man of valor,"* who carried the potential to lead three hundred men to victory over hundreds of thousands, was going under cover of darkness to do this first, tiny assignment — for fear of being killed by those he was called to deliver. However, it now became apparent why God had called Gideon *"a mighty man of valor."* He obeyed. When we are willing to obey God, He can turn our timid obedience into a mighty display of His power. Gideon was fearful at every step in the process, but he was also obedient in every step of the process. We can conclude from this that it is more important to obey than to feel confident. If we obey, confidence will come. This confidence is not in ourselves, but it's a confidence in the Lord. This also defines what true faith is.

> *But the Spirit of the Lord came upon Gideon; then he blew the trumpet, and the Abiezrites gathered behind him.* Judges 6:34

The Abiezrites were Gideon's own people, and when they saw that he had knocked over the image of Baal and nothing happened to him, they were released from the fear of that false god. Baal, apparently, was the one thing Gideon did not fear.

The Spirit of the Lord was now upon Gideon, and he gathered a host of followers by these two acts — knocking over an altar to a false god and blowing a trumpet. Was he now convinced that he was God's man for the hour? Not hardly:

> *Then Gideon said to God, "If you will save Israel by my hand as You have said — "look I shall put a fleece of wool on the threshing floor; if there is dew on the fleece only, and it is dry on all the ground, then I shall know that You will save Israel by my hand, as you have said."*
>
> *And it was so. When he rose early the next morning and squeezed the fleece together, he wrung the dew out of the fleece, a bowl full of water.*
>
> *Then Gideon said to God, "Do not be angry with me, and let me speak just once more: Let me test, I pray, just once more with the fleece; let it now be dry only on the fleece, but on all the ground let there be dew."*
>
> *And God did so that night. It was dry on the fleece only, but there was dew on all the ground.* Judges 6:36-40

Gideon had now seen the Lord, had seen fire come from a rock, had watched the Lord vanish in front of his very eyes, had blown a trumpet and had seen a multitude of people come out to follow him. The Lord had already promised him victory, but still he sought more confirmation. In this passage, he reminded the Lord twice about saying that He would save Israel by his hand. He wanted to make double sure he hadn't heard wrong.

This Gideon is not someone we should strive to emulate, but God doesn't hide just how weak, small and foolish that he was. And if He can find a weak person who will obey Him today, He will release great power through that person — just as He did with Gideon.

There is more to Gideon's story. As we review it, allow the Holy Spirit to strip away the layers of burial clothes that bind you and let your spirit be unleashed to accomplish great things for God:

The Lord Is With You, Mighty Man!

And the Lord said to Gideon, "The people who are with you are too many for Me to give the Midianites into their hands, lest Israel claim glory for itself against Me, saying, 'My own hand has saved me.' " Judges 7:2

This verse is an important one. It says so much about the way our Lord works. It confirms the pattern we are seeing throughout the Scriptures. This is not an isolated truth. God wants to help us win, but He wants to do it in a way that will bring Him glory. We cannot think that victory comes because of us. If we have an ability to win, then God must humble us — until we know that we cannot win without His help. If we have confidence in our numbers, then He must subtract from those numbers — until all the glory is His.

Again, God spoke to Gideon:

Now therefore, proclaim in the hearing of the people, saying, "Whoever is fearful and afraid, let him turn and depart at once from Mount Gilead." And twenty-two thousand of the people returned, and ten thousand remained. Judges 7:3

If the Lord wanted to get rid of all the fearful men, would that not have disqualified Gideon himself? After all, he had been fearful at every turn. The difference seems to be that Gideon had never deserted. In spite of his fears, he continued to be obedient. The final proof of disabling fear is quitting, and Gideon didn't quit. Many went home that day, and Gideon was left with far fewer soldiers.

Then God spoke again:

And the Lord said to Gideon, "The people are still too many; bring them down to the water, and I will test them for you there. Then it will be, that of whom I say to you, 'This one shall go with you,' the same shall go with you; and of whomsoever I say to you, 'This one shall not go with you,' the same shall not go." Judges 7:4

In this way, even more men were eliminated from Gideon's army. God was narrowing it down, lessening the numbers, so that neither

Gideon nor his men could have confidence in their ability to win without His help.

The numbers would soon dwindle further:

So he brought the people down to the water. And the Lord said to Gideon, "Everyone who laps from the water with his tongue, as a dog laps, you shall set apart by himself; likewise everyone who gets down on his knees to drink." And the number of those who lapped, putting their hand to their mouth, was three hundred men; but all the rest of the people got down on their knees to drink water. Then the Lord said to Gideon, "By the three hundred men who lapped I will save you, and deliver the Midianites into your hand. Let all the other people go, every man to his place."

So the people took provisions and their trumpets in their hands. And he sent away all the rest of Israel, every man to his tent, and retained those three hundred men. Now the camp of Midian was below him in the valley. And it happened on the same night that the Lord said to him, "Arise, go down against the camp, for I have delivered it into your hand."

Judges 7:5-9

Much has been preached and taught on Gideon's three hundred and the symbolism of those who were sent home and those who remained. The three hundred men, however, should not be our focus. By whittling the men down to three hundred, the Lord wasn't saying that He needed quality over quantity. Though it makes for great preaching, the men who remained with Gideon did not need to be special at all. They were not needed to fight the battle; God would do that.

When it did come time to fight, the Scriptures say, *"And every man stood in his place all around the camp"* (Judges 7:21). When they did this, God did the work: *"The Lord set every man's sword against his companion throughout the whole camp"* (verse 22). We have thought of the three hundred who lapped the water as representing a higher level of alertness that the Lord must have desired. Again, it makes for good preaching, but if it was true, the heightened alertness of these men was never utilized. They blew trumpets and smashed pitchers and yelled, *"The sword of the Lord and of Gideon"* (verse 20). That was not a very sophisticated battle plan!

As an experiment, try drinking as the two groups of men did. Put some water in your hand and drink from it. Then picture how a dog laps water and try that. You might not want to do it in public, for you would look rather foolish. But was that the very reason the Lord chose these men? Were they willing to look foolish before others? Were they untouched by *"the fear of men"*? The Lord hadn't told Gideon simply to choose those who lapped, but those who lapped like a dog. It was a totally "uncool" way to drink, and only three hundred out of ten thousand did it that way, probably while being snickered at.

The Lord was intent on keeping Gideon's focus off of man. If he was to learn how to have victory, his focus needed to stay on God. When obedient men are willing to do foolish things, God is able to release His strength. God is not looking for heavy thinkers; He is looking for obedient servants. Heavy thinkers believe that they must help the Lord. They have a hard time standing still while the Holy Spirit is moving and destroying the enemy.

For sure, Gideon's three hundred were special — but not in the way we think of specialness. Traditionally, we have thought of them as valiant warriors, but they were just obedient servants.

The enemy they faced that day was formidable. They were *"as numerous as locusts,"* and their camels were *"as the sand by the seashore in multitude"* (Judges 7:12). Only men who trusted God would not worry about odds like those.

Gideon set the men in position and armed them:

> *Then he divided the three hundred men into three companies, and he put a trumpet into every man's hand, with empty pitchers, and torches inside the pitchers.*   Judges 7:16

No normal soldier would have accepted this fighting gear. And can you imagine splitting such a small contingent into three companies? As if the odds were not already bad enough, now they were going to attempt to surround an innumerable army with three small bands of a hundred soldiers each. This was unheard of!

Some have said that it was the trumpet blasts that frightened the enemy into killing their fellow soldiers. That could have happened, but it is not exactly what the Scriptures say:

> *When the three hundred blew the trumpets, the Lord set every man's sword against his companion throughout the whole camp.*   Judges 7:22

The trumpets did something, but it was not to intimidate the enemy. What the trumpets did was to set in motion the work the Lord had determined upon the enemy. It was this act of obedience that loosed the hand of God to work. The trumpet sound was a sign that there was a remnant that still believed that the battle was the Lord's and not their own. That trumpet sound meant, "We are willing to do it Your way, Lord. We may look rather foolish, and we are certainly weak, but we will obey You nevertheless."

I believe we will see this story replayed many times as a part of the prophetic picture in these last days. God will use small bands of radically obedient fools to achieve enormous victories. These bands will exhaust themselves pursuing and slaying the enemy. They will do these exploits with trumpets and with pitchers with fire. Symbolically, trumpets are the proclamation of the Lord's intentions. Pitchers with fire, which have been broken, symbolize fire that is no longer hidden.

JOSHUA AT JERICHO

Joshua and the battle of Jericho is another well-known Bible story. Sometimes familiarity breeds contempt. Let us look at the story as if we are seeing it for the very first time.

What took place in the early chapters of Joshua was a preparation for what was to happen at Jericho. The children of Israel, now a whole new generation, had to first cross the Jordan River before they could even have a chance at Jericho. Joshua and Caleb were the only ones among them who had seen the Red Sea parted. Although every Israelite had heard of that miracle, virtually none of them had been personally exposed to this level of the supernatural. If it had been us, of course, we would have tried extending our rods over the Jordan until it parted. That was how Moses had done it. "And we must stick with what works," many say. Since the Lord is God, however, He gives Himself the freedom to do things differently.

The Lord told Joshua:

> *And it shall come to pass, as soon as the soles of the feet of the priests who bear the ark of the Lord, the Lord of all the earth, shall rest in the waters of the Jordan, that the waters of the Jordan shall be cut off, the waters that come down from upstream, and they shall stand as a heap.*
>
> Joshua 3:13

This fresh revelation was obeyed, and sure enough, the people were able to cross the Jordan River on dry ground. This experience, however, was not identical to the Red Sea crossing. This time, someone had to start walking on the water first. Then the miracle came. Although this violated all scriptural precedents and was not the way Moses had done it, the people obeyed the voice of the Lord — and it worked. In this way, this new generation of Israelites learned that Joshua was also hearing from the Lord — even if what God was saying was not the "Moses way" of doing things. There was now a "Joshua way" of doing things:

> *On that day the Lord magnified Joshua in the sight of all Israel; and they feared him as they feared Moses, all the days of his life.*   Joshua 3:14

That day, some issues, significant for the long-term, were being established by the Lord. The current generation had more than a past glory of which to speak. They now had a personal story to tell. All this also served to establish Joshua's leadership in the sight of the people.

There was another important outcome to this miracle:

So it was, when all the kings of the Amorites who were on the west side of the Jordan, and all the kings of the Canaanites who were by the sea, heard that the Lord had dried up the waters of the Jordan from before the children of Israel until we had crossed over, that their heart melted; and there was no spirit in them any longer because of the children of Israel.

Joshua 5:1

When God moves mightily in our midst, the often under-reported effect is what it does to our enemies. God's power in demonstration among us forces the enemy to take defensive measures, causing the enemy to cease offensive tactics. I believe that the Lord is about to release an imposing end-time dread into the heart of the enemy through some of the awesome signs and wonders He is going to do. In fact, I am already seeing it happen.

Joshua marched on toward Jericho:

Now Jericho was securely shut up because of the children of Israel; none went out, and none came in. And the Lord said to Joshua: "See! I have given Jericho into your hand, its king, and the mighty men of valor. You shall march around the city, all you men of war; you shall go all around the city once. This shall you do six days. And seven priests shall bear seven trumpets of rams' horns before the ark. But the seventh day you shall march around the city seven times, and the priests shall blow the trumpets. Then it shall come to pass, when they make a long blast with the ram's horn, and when you hear the sound of the trumpet, that all the people shall shout with a great shout; then the wall of the city will fall down flat. And the people shall go up every man straight up before him." Joshua 6:1-5

The people of Jericho were already in fear of the Israelites, and this is difficult to explain in the natural. Jericho had more than one wall. There was one forty-foot wall that ran all the way around the city, and it was wide enough for a chariot to run on. There was also a moat outside that wall, and then there was another wall, identical to the first, outside of that. This made the city seem like an impregnable fortress. How could such a city be taken?

Today, in our modern approach to "taking over," we would have gone to a more direct cause-and-effect effort. We would have strategically placed dynamite and other explosives at key locations around the city. This is the type of approach that we basically bring to most of our "Christian agenda" issues.

Consider the following analogies for a moment: Are we really going to rid our country of homosexuality through demonstrations, marches, and banners against it? Or, in the case of abortion, is changing the law the true key in eliminating abortions? Fortunately, most people have totally rejected the "solution" that bombing clinics brings. However, by and large, we as Christians resort much too quickly to protests, boycotting, and voting as our primary modern-day weaponry. I do not wish to deny anyone the right or responsibility of good citizenship. I believe that we should do what we can in this arena. However, we cannot lean upon this course of action as a basic church strategy. Spiritual weapons, which go to the heart of issues, are released when we obey God's "today" directives.

The weapons of our warfare are not carnal but mighty in God for pulling down strongholds.   2 Corinthians 10:4

Our weapons are *"mighty in God."* There is no problem that is too big to be approached with a spiritual weapon, and the most underappreciated weapon of power at our disposal is simple obedience.

The battle is always *"the Lord's,"* and He moves through very unsophisticated acts of obedience. He often does things through prophetic symbolism, and He always has a reason for what He is doing. There is a reason that God is bringing back the trumpet, the marching and the shouting to His people. They are all significant in the Spirit realm. They also remind us of Joshua and how easy it can be to do the impossible — from crossing the Jordan to taking impenetrable double-walled cities.

However, should all our trumpets be confiscated so that we cannot blow them, should all our legs be broken so that we cannot march, and should all of us get laryngitis so that we cannot shout, the battle can still be won. These are only tools of obedience, and God can easily supply others. Blowing a trumpet does not carry intrinsic value of its own. It was the obedience in the act that produced the supernatural effect.

The Lord used Balaam's donkey to give him an important message, but you don't need to rush out and buy a donkey of your own. Samson used the jawbone of such an animal to kill a thousand Philistines, and Jesus made His Triumphal Entry into the city of Jerusalem on the back of one of them, but that doesn't imply that we would all be better served or empowered if we bought our own personal donkeys. The issue is the obedience involved.

We notice many "sevens" in Joshua chapter 6. There were seven priests, seven trumpets, seven days and seven times. Numbers are very significant in the Scriptures. Each one has symbolic meaning. God might ask us to do any number of things in any number of ways. Obedience is always the key. One reason we are often asked to do things in sevens is due to the deep significance the number has.

God created the world in seven days. There were seven churches in Revelation to which John was instructed to write. Naaman the leper dipped seven times in the Jordan River and was totally healed. The theme of sevens runs throughout the Bible.

Seven means "full, or complete." Though it is an exact number itself, it is also representative of something that has reached fullness or maturation. When Jesus told Peter that he was to forgive *"seventy times seven"* (Matthew 18:22), He didn't literally mean that he should forgive four hundred and ninety times. He meant that Peter should forgive until the work was done in him. In the same way, the Lord often has us do things seven times to bring about a moment of divine intervention.

Six is the number of man, and it represents man's ways, man's efforts and man's methodology. Man was created on the sixth day. The number of the anti-Christ is 666, representing the fullness of man's thoughts, man's words and man's behavior. Seven is the number of God's intervention. It comes after we have run out of man's options for getting something accomplished and must rely on the supernatural.

This is important in the story of Joshua. By using the symbolism of the number seven over and over again in this story, the Lord is showing us that the supernatural was taking over. As we are called in the days ahead to do various foolish acts seven times, let us remember the significance of this number. When we do something seven times, we are admitting our inability to get something done without the Lord, and we are also fully comprehending His ability to do the job without us.

From a power standpoint, God does not need us. He is fully capable of getting anything done that He wishes to get done of His own accord. However, He has chosen to need us. In many areas, He has limited Himself to what we activate, or loose, Him to do. It is His apparent nature to always use something to make something else. He didn't just make man out of nothing, though He could have. He formed man from the dust. Likewise, when He made Eve, He started with Adam's rib.

When Jesus came to Earth, He manifested this same divine attribute. He healed the blind man — using spit and the mud He made with His spit to heal the man's eyes. When He fed the five thousand, He could have done it without anyone's lunch, but He chose to limit Himself to beginning with something that existed. Therefore, He used the five loaves and two fishes a lad had brought, and with them, He did that great miracle.

We must never refrain from doing some act of obedience simply because it seems too insignificant. Many think, "Well, if God wants to do it, He'll just do it anyway." That's not true, for He has chosen to limit Himself to our small insignificant acts of obedience.

In June of 1999, the Lord sent a team of twelve of us from two churches to the city of Cuzco, Peru, for intercession. We had invitations to speak, and there were other things we could have done to make ourselves feel that we had accomplished something, but the Lord had us respond to the Spirit rather than to our minds. For two days, we did nothing but move around Cuzco and Macchu Picchu (the lost city of the Incas) interceding before the throne of God.

During those days, we marched around many things seven times. We laid hands on altars dedicated to demons of death and violence and broke every historic demonic pact that the Lord revealed to us.

Cuzco has come to be considered as the New Age capital of the world, replacing even Llasa in Tibet. Because it was historically a site of human sacrifices, shamans and other occult figures often said that they feel "great energy" in the area. Churches, on the other hand, have not done well in the Cuzco area. The Lord showed us through dreams and visions that there were spiritual strongholds over the entire country of Peru that were energized through the on-going idolatry and resident curses of the Cuzco/Macchu Picchu area.

Because we *"see in part,"* we have no way of knowing the extent of what we accomplished during our two days there. However, we believe it was significant and that God has begun a plan of intervention. We know that there have been many other prayers of intercession over that place, and we joined ours with them. We neither want to overestimate how the Lord used us there nor underestimate what He accomplished. As I'm pointing out over and over again, He only needs small acts of obedience to unleash powerful nation-rattling interventions.

Peru has been beset by violence throughout its history. Within days of our intercessory trip, the country's most wanted rebel, Feliciano, was captured. He was the remaining leader of the violent Shining Path guerrillas and had been on the run (and still killing) since 1992. He was only a small piece of the puzzle for that country, but through this, the Lord showed me that our acts of foolish obedience helped to bring to the surface an important architect of evildoing there.

The fact that something happened so quickly and visibly strengthened our faith. From the reports I'm receiving, there are also spiritual breakthroughs occurring all over the country. I expect to soon hear about sustained uncontrollable wildfires of God's revival in that land.

Am I over-crediting our trip to Cuzco? Maybe — but only eternity will tell. All I know is that when I pray, I pray believing. I assume that we are small, weak and foolish enough that God could be doing something really big through us — as He has done through others in the past.

Joshua set forth:

> *So Joshua the son of Nun called the priests and said to them, "Take up the ark of the covenant, and let seven priests bear seven trumpets of rams' horns before the ark of the Lord." And he said to the people, "Proceed, and march around the city, and let him who is armed advance before the ark of the Lord."*
>
> *So it was, when Joshua had spoken to the people, that the seven priests bearing the seven trumpets of rams' horns before the Lord advanced and blew the trumpets, and the ark of the covenant of the Lord followed them. The armed men went before the priests who blew the trumpets, and the rear guard came after the ark, while the priests continued blowing the trumpets.*
>
> *Now Joshua had commanded the people, saying, "You shall not shout or make any noise with your voice, nor shall any word proceed out of your mouth, until the day I say to you, 'Shout!' Then you shall shout."*
>
> *So he had the ark of the Lord circle the city, going around it once. Then they came into the camp and lodged in the camp.*   Joshua 6:6-11

The procedure that God outlined for the people was followed for seven days in a row. It has been said that the miracle here was that several hundred thousand people could remain absolutely quiet for so long.

This march around the city was no quick jaunt. At the very least, it took several hours, and during that time, no words were spoken over a period of seven days. What a miracle! I believe that what Israel was doing was so obviously foolish that Joshua needed to squelch the release of doubt and unbelief. If the people had been allowed to talk, the first thing out of their mouths would have been something like, "Isn't this ridiculous?" Their silence prevented mutiny from occurring.

Even for those who remembered the recent parting of the Jordan River, this march must have seemed strange. They knew what was supposed to happen at the river, but here, they were unsure of what to expect.

Joshua had not told the people exactly what to expect, and there was a reason for that. The walls of Jericho coming down was such an unbelievable phenomenon that he apparently thought it best to keep it to himself. The marchers were probably expecting something to happen to the gates of the city. This would have been a more "reasonable" miracle. Perhaps they envisioned the gates suddenly splitting in two.

By the seventh day, though, nothing had happened. This day, they marched around the city seven times, rather than just one. When Joshua gave the instruction for everyone to shout, they must have been exhausted. It was already late in the day, and they were all at their weakest. It had been a hard week, after all. But it was at this moment of their lowest ebb that God chose to work (and this should not surprise us):

So the people shouted when the priests blew the trumpets. And it happened when the people heard the sound of the trumpet, and the people shouted with a great shout, that the wall went down flat. Then the people went up into the city, every man straight before him, and they took the city.

Joshua 6:20

Another of the miracles of this story is that the walls *"fell down flat."* What exactly happened, we don't know. The walls either disintegrated, or they sunk into the ground. In a moment's time, what had been considered an impassable obstacle was now virtually untraceable. In one moment's time, the enemy's defense system was totally leveled.

This is also a prophetic word for us today. We are a "seventh" people, and there is a maturation of many things taking place in us today. We are marching around the city on the final day, and we must be ready for the huge holes the Lord will make in the enemy's defenses. We must be positioned to invade places we have never before invaded, and we must be ready to totally destroy the enemy and his bulwarks.

Walls will begin to come down right in front of us, and we must march straight ahead into the cities that become opened to us to possess. There are walled cities we have not even begun to invade because of our fear of being polluted by them. For example, there is an enormous sex cesspool underworld that we have avoided until now so as not to be contaminated by it. There are literally millions of human beings on this planet who are in bondage to the sex trade. We encourage everyone we know to avoid the cesspools of pornography, but what of the tens of thousands of young women who are forced into this trade and into prostitution? Hundreds of thousands of otherwise good mothers have been forced into prostitution for economic reasons.

Many of those who are involved in the vast sex trade are there because at some point they were victims themselves. There is a huge underworld of pedophilia, and we in the Church have had no idea how to invade this world to rescue those who are bound by it. There is an underworld of bestiality that has as yet gone unchallenged by the Church. We consider the homosexual underworld to be much too disgusting for us to approach. And the list goes on and on. By staying away from all these evils, avoiding the pollution they could bring us, we continue to allow this ever-growing, rushing river of filth to erode our younger generations.

This evil is much more vast than most of us care to know. In the deep jungles of Peru, where people are thin for lack of food, hardcore pornography can be received on normal television channels for everyone to view. A friend told me that in Albania two of the four television channels that can be received air hard-core pornography. Around the world, our younger generations are routinely exposed to very obscene, hard-core pornography over the Internet. It is not just nudity; it is degrading perversion.

Personally, I don't know yet how we will deal with all this. The pollution seems too much for us. I just know that at some point we must address it. Isaiah declared that we are *"to proclaim liberty to the captives, and the opening of the prison to those who are bound"* (Isaiah 61:1). This does not exclude those who happen to be in sexual prisons. Jesus died just as much for the sexual slaves as He did for the slave to anything else.

It is very possible that the Lord will raise up an army of holy women, who, with spiritual strategies, will invade this evil world that seems to be so much more perilous for men. Something must be done. This is a BIG problem. We Americans may incur serious judgment as a nation for this one issue alone if we are not able somehow, through the Spirit, to stem the tide of vileness. I believe that we will be called upon to release the judgment of the Lord upon this industry — if only to deter some of the judgment upon us as a country.

This walled city is ominous, but God has a plan. The battle is the Lord's. We just need to find the small areas of obedience that will unleash His power to the world around us in each battle or circumstance we face. Thus, we can become the Joshuas of our day.

Rise up, Gideons, Joshuas, mighty men and women of the twenty-first century, and take your place!

CHAPTER 7

GREATER WORKS THAN THESE

Most assuredly, I say to you, he who believes in Me, the works that I do he will do also; and greater works than these he will do, because I go to My Father.   John 14:12

Do these truths work today in our modern world? They do.

In July of 1999, I took a short trip with my brother-in-law, Jim, to Tingo Maria, Peru, for two days of meetings in a church there. We had both lived in that city (for about five years) more than twenty years before. This was my first trip back as a minister. We had meetings during the day and two special nightly meetings.

Our nightly meetings were held in a small, partially-open coliseum. We had a decent turnout the first night, and the Lord did a few neat things. Fairly early, however, we realized that there seemed to be some demonic opposition to this meeting. This became apparent when, during worship, someone began throwing rocks over the back walls into the crowd. A man who was about ten feet from me was struck in the head and went down with a bloody wound. He had to be taken out of the meeting and attended to.

When this happened, the young pastor of the church got up to the microphone and yelled out, "We just want to tell whoever is throwing the rocks that we love you." He also had the congregation shout out loud together that they loved the stone throwers. It was the correct response and a great witness.

Later, when I was preaching, someone decided to have a party outside, and they put on some loud blaring music. To overcome the effect of this music, I had to speak very loud. Even then, it was difficult to keep the people focused on the message. The entire night seemed to be like that, an exercise in pressing through.

Jim had felt that we should determine the center of the city and do some marching and interceding there. (This is something we often do.) I spoke with the local pastors about doing that, and they readily agreed that we should march around the central plaza.

As it turned out, one of the pastors had just completed a study of the original architecture of the central plaza area and had discovered that, at its inception, Tingo Maria had been dedicated to death and sexual perversion. He took us on a little tour through the three central blocks of town and pointed out the symbols, statues and altars set up by the founder of the city.

That central area of the city faces a mountain now called *La Bella Durmiente* (Sleeping Beauty). It is one of the main tourist attractions of Tingo Maria. As you view the mountain from the center of town, it looks like a woman lying on her back sleeping. What we hadn't known was the fact that when the city was built, the idea of "Sleeping Beauty" did not yet exist. The founder of Tingo Maria had called the mountain *La Mujer Degollada*, or "The Woman With the Slit Throat." The central area of town had been set up as a ceremonial viewing area for this dead woman.

There were also some very sexually explicit symbols scattered throughout the central plaza area. Suddenly, everything about Tingo Maria, past and present, made sense.

Tingo Maria is not in a highly-accessible part of Peru. It is at the edge of the jungle, and it takes about twelve hours by bus to reach it from Lima. At one time, the town was the world leader in cocaine production. How interesting that a place dedicated to death should become the leading exporter of death through drugs!

There was more. During the reign of terror of the Marxist guerilla group "Shining Path," Tingo Maria had been at the center of much of the violence. Only Ayacucho (the headquarters of the movement) saw more violence. We learned that more than fifty of our immediate neighbors (when we had lived there twenty years before) had been killed by the Shining Path, often in horrific fashion. Eight different mayors of Tingo Maria had been killed by guerrillas. Interestingly enough, the office of the mayor was located right in the middle of all this occultic architectural symbolism.

Tingo Maria was a "city of death," and we were shown sites where it was said that witch doctors continued making sacrifices to the gods of death.

Through the years, Tingo Maria has been notorious for its prostitution, as well as for fornication, adultery and other forms of sexual impurity. Although these evils exist nearly everywhere, the scope of these activities was unusually intense in Tingo Maria, and even the leaders of churches had been affected.

On our second day in Tingo Maria, we set out to march around the central area of the city seven times and to finish the march with seven times around the central plaza. There were about a hundred of us (mostly young people from the churches), and we lined up two-by-two. One of the young men had brought a guitar, and as we marched in the midday heat, we sang *Jehovah Es Mi Guerrero*, "The Lord Is My Warrior," a good marching song.

While we marched and sang that day, we sensed that something powerful was being unleashed. It wasn't logical, but it was biblical. Angels were being released to work in the city. We broke all covenants that had been made with demons. We laid our hands on the various statues and altars and renounced the power they had held. (This called to mind Gideon being sent to dethrone Baal.)

As we were doing this, two demonized individuals suddenly appeared in the marching area. It was apparent that they wanted to disrupt us. I looked at them sternly and shook my head. They were clearly agitated, but they were unable to do anything to hinder us. We were able to finish our march unimpeded.

The march lasted for more than an hour, and as we finished, we all let out a very powerful shout to the Lord. To those who were observing us, we might have appeared crazy (as happened when Gideon's three hundred blew their trumpets and broke their pitchers). It did seem foolish to believe that all this was accomplishing anything. That night, however, it was apparent that it had.

For one thing, we had a full house. There were about twice as many people in the meeting that night as had been there the night before. And this time, we had no interruptions at all. There was also an unbelievable new freedom in the worship.

People came that night from churches that hadn't met together for years because of past disputes, and there was a wave of reconciliation among them during the worship time. People who hadn't spoken to each other in years began hugging one another and weeping.

I called the youth leader from one of the churches up to the platform and began to prophesy over him. I told him a fresh anointing from God was about to fall upon him and the rest of the young people. I had not yet touched him, but as I said this, he fell backward onto the floor. The power of God was suddenly flowing without the previous night's restriction.

When we came to the ministry time toward the end of the meeting, it got even better. The first five people I prayed over were instantly healed. Many Peruvians cannot afford to have their physical problems diagnosed, and their healing is determined by the fact that they feel the power of God going through their bodies and the area that previously hurt no longer hurts. That's how we determined the healings. Others were delivered from depressions and oppressions, as demons had to flee.

Young children came to the front requesting to receive the baptism in the Holy Spirit. As we spoke the words, "Holy Spirit, baptize them," they immediately fell backward (as if they were literally being baptized). The Holy Spirit was revealing His power in many different ways. There was crying, laughing and shaking taking place simultaneously all over the building.

As the meeting ended, ten young men walked in off the street that night looking for the Lord. Jim was able to lead them all to the feet of Jesus. Others had already been led to the Lord in the course of the meeting.

Near midnight, I was finally leaving the building, when a young lady arrived and asked if I would pray for her. She was the director of a Christian arts ministry (dance and drama) in Lima. She was in the city for another meeting, and someone had told her about the wonderful things happening in the little coliseum. I prayed for her, and the Lord gave me some prophetic words for her. She began to shake from head to toe. Then, all of a sudden, she broke out in a beautiful, unrehearsed dance unto the Lord. She moved back and forth with her eyes closed, clearly under the inspiration of the Holy Spirit. This went on for some twenty or thirty minutes.

This young lady, Maria, has e-mailed me several times since that night. She said that she will never forget the special things the Lord did for her that night and the encouraging things He said to her. As a pioneer in her type of ministry, she faces much opposition. I'm looking forward to seeing what the Lord does with her in the future.

My friend, Edgar, oversees the work in Tingo Maria, though he himself lives in Huanuco. He told me that the spiritual atmosphere over Tingo Maria has changed dramatically since those days. Several other pastors have called him and thanked him for what we did in the city. To show their gratitude, they suggested that they take all their young people and help do the same thing in Huanuco. I'm sure we'll hear great reports from that effort. They now have a plan to go city by city along the course of the Andes Mountains to do intercessory marches and "Baal tossings," as the Lord leads them.

It sounds like there was some immediate fruit from our Gideonic acts of foolishness. This is not to say that the people of Tingo Maria will face no future battles. They will have more wars, but they will be won the same way.

We still do not know all the long-term effects of our obedience, and sometimes there are no immediate results that encourage us that things are indeed different. The Lord was good to us in Tingo Maria. Sometimes we just add to the cup of righteousness and empty from the cup of iniquity; the levels in both cups are being constantly changed, and sometimes we can make the good cup instantly tip through small acts of apparent foolishness.

Did we just copy the "seven-times march" formula from Joshua and Jericho? No, we got ours in the same way they got theirs. The Holy Spirit caused us to perform this biblical act to stir our faith. The Lord might just as easily have led us to roll or somersault around the city and thus release His power, but most of us are afraid to do something that is not precisely outlined in the Bible. We fail to recognize that the Holy Spirit is not giving a model or formula, but rather a creative example of obedience.

Should raising a rod over a body of sea water cause it to part? It did in Moses' case. Should Aaron and Hur holding up Moses' hands on a mountain cause the victory to be won in the valley below? It did in that case. Should striking a rock with a rod cause water to come forth? It worked for Moses. Notice, however, that God didn't want Moses to get water the same way the next time. This time, he was to speak to the rock. God was not interested in us being able to develop a "water from the rock" formula. The theological formula is obedience.

Why was Gideon able to get away with just blowing the trumpets, when Joshua had been required to march around the city? Why didn't Joshua just climb up a nearby mountain and have somebody hold his hands up? If a person has leprosy, can they be healed only by dipping in the Jordan River? It worked for Naaman.

Even in the ministry of Jesus, we see the variety of methods. Is spitting and making mud and then putting it into someone's eyes the only correct way to heal blindness? Why did He lay hands sometimes, just speak sometimes, spit sometimes, breathe sometimes, forgive sins sometimes, rebuke the illness sometimes, and say, "It's already done," sometimes? Is He not doing something more than approving models of healing? As we read in Genesis 1:1, *"In the beginning God created... ."* He is first revealed to us, not as a copier, but as a creator. He is the God of creation, and He continues to do things in creative ways. He is not the great "I Was," but the great I AM. His work is new, alive and fresh.

Those who war against Him have always aimed at squelching Him and His freedom from traditions. We have the example of the Pharisees and their need to see uniformity in order to feel spiritual.

Then the scribes and Pharisees who were from Jerusalem came to Jesus, saying, "Why do Your disciples transgress the tradition of the elders? For they do not wash their hands when they eat bread."
But He answered and said to them, "Why do you also transgress the commandment of God because of your tradition?"   Matthew 15:1-3

This same spirit is at work today. When people ask, "Where do you find that in the Scriptures?" their question is motivated by that same spirit of phariseeism. If that question is asked about the propagation of a new doctrine, it may well be a legitimate question. If it has anything to do with methodology or manifestation, it becomes illegitimate. Our traditions have caused us to transgress against God.

What is "tradition" anyway? The word *tradition* means "the way a thing has always been done." It is easy to see that "tradition" and the Holy Spirit are rarely going to get along.

Now the Lord is the Spirit; and where the Spirit of the Lord is, there is liberty.   2 Corinthians 3:17

Every believer who desires to do God's will should memorize this verse. Liberty is the antithesis of tradition. If you look up the word *liberty* in Webster's Dictionary, here are some of the definitions you will find: "the quality or state of being free; freedom from arbitrary or despotic control; the positive enjoyment of various ... rights and privileges; the power of choice."

Based on what the Scriptures say about liberty, we could say: "Now Pharisees are traditionalists; and where traditionalists are, there is bondage." Creativity is an indication that the Holy Spirit is at work. Our problem today is that every time the Holy Spirit breaks through with something new, we copycat it to death. To the degree that we formulize something, to that degree we lose the power of it. Where the Spirit of the Lord is, there is freedom.

A formula is an arbitrary control mechanism. Where the Spirit of the Lord is, there is no arbitrary control mechanism. The Lord can reignite something that has been previously done, but any repetition that does not have the Lord as its source will soon become a bondage.

I am aware that there are potential excesses in everything. There are people who are actually in bondage to being free, and there are people who excuse their own "bizarreness" under the label of liberty. Satan tries to use excess to totally eradicate the balance that God desires to have present in our meetings. Having said that, I must say that the lack of freedom and creativity is by far our greater problem. To those who would nod their head to this, remembering something bizarre they have seen, I would say this: If you did not discern it by the Spirit, you really have no idea if it was "bizarre" or not. It might have been totally anointed by the Holy Spirit. Remember, *"The natural man receives not the things of the Spirit of God ... nor can he know them for they are spiritually discerned"* (1 Corinthians 2:14).

I have been doing a lot of shouting, marching and trumpet-blowing recently, and I have seen great fruit from it. I feel that I have a general word from the Lord that if I do any of these three things in faith, He will move. There are times when the Lord strongly moves on me to shout, and I do it. On more than one occasion, the Lord has used that as the vehicle for releasing His Spirit upon others.

I have sometimes gone down a prayer line and just yelled into the stomach area of the people. As I have done that strange thing, some people have collapsed to the floor, shaking like a leaf. Others have burst into tears. Others have been overwhelmed with uncontrollable joy. It seems that the Holy Spirit has taken that prophetic act as His cue to demonstrate His power.

We might formulate from that experience a theology for the need to yell into someone's stomach, but then how could I explain the fact that I shouted into one pastor's back, and he collapsed and lay there for three hours, unable to get up? He cried virtually the entire time, and the Lord gave him some important direction for His movement in South America during that "downtime."

The biblical trumpets were actually rams' horns, which are nowadays called *shofars*. I enjoy blowing shofars (not because I'm good at it). Sometimes, when I blow a shofar, what comes out sounds like a sick elephant. I've learned, however, that the Lord doesn't respond to the excellence of the sound, but to our faith and obedience. In my own case, I rarely actually hear the Lord telling me to blow the shofar. Usually, I ask His permission to blow it, and He gives me the okay.

After one meeting at a pastors' conference in Huanuco, Peru, a young pastor came to me and asked if I could have a special prayer over him. I suddenly felt inspired to blow my shofar, and I blew it again and again. While I was doing this, the pastor was visibly hit by the power of God. On the floor that day, he had the encounter with God he had been desiring.

Another good example of victory obtained through marching occurred in Lima, Peru. Our team of six men was staying in a hotel on the Plaza San Martín in the center of the city. We had just come back from a rewarding, but exhausting, trip to the jungle. We were scheduled to go to Cuzco the next day, and this was our night off. At about nine o'clock that night, we decided to go to the center of the plaza (right outside our window) and do a few minutes of intercession over the city and the country before we retired for the night. When we got down to the statue of José de San Martín, the revolutionary South American leader, one of our team members named Frank suggested that we march around the statue seven times as we prayed. This would not take long, and it seemed to inspire faith in us.

As we marched the first time around, we began to proclaim the Lordship of Jesus over Peru and to thank Him for the many things He had already done on the trip. We proclaimed a harvest of souls within the country and a move of God in the entire area. Two of the men, Scott (the van-lifter) and Jim (my brother-in-law), asked the Lord to give us a sign that He was going to do what we were declaring. They asked to confirm that He had heard our cry by granting us a soul before we went back to the hotel (those two never seem to be concerned with sleep anyway).

Until that moment, there had been no one else in sight. However, as we made the next turn around the statue, two young men appeared. Scott and Jim signaled to the rest of us that they were going to deal with these young men and that we should keep on marching. By the time we had circled the statue one more time these two young men came up to me and said that they had just accepted the Lord into their hearts. We had a double portion of the sign we asked for, and we had not yet finished circling seven times.

By the time we had finished walking around the statue, a small crowd had gathered. There was no apparent reason. Foreigners are commonplace in Lima, and we had been fairly quiet as we marched. We were not creating a scene in any sense of the word.

I was exhausted and wanted to get back to the hotel and get some rest, but again, the Lord showed that when we are weak, He is strong. Soon, I was fielding questions about who we were and what we were doing. I tried to hurry the conversations along, for I was not in the mood for late-night evangelism, but one thing led to another, and before long, it was apparent that the man I was talking with wanted to know Jesus. When I asked him if this was true, he nodded his head in assent. There, in front of everyone, he boldly made his profession of faith, repeating after me as I prayed.

I still wasn't getting into the thing, but then another young man about ten feet from me blurted out, "I feel something right here," and he patted his heart.

I asked, "Is it good? Or is it bad."

"It's good," he responded. "I was standing back there a little ways, and I was thinking, *What a bunch of lies!* Then I moved in closer, and I was just hit with this feeling."

"Do you want to receive Jesus into your heart?" I asked.

"Yes, I do," he replied, and we prayed out loud together again.

I asked both of these young men how they felt, and they both answered that they now felt an incredible peace.

I still had not preached a thing; I was only answering questions. Most of the instruction I had been able to give was done as I was leading each of the individuals in a sinner's prayer. Then, suddenly, another young man had something he wanted to say. "I feel anxious," he blurted out.

"Anxious about your life?" I asked.

The young man nodded.

"Do you wish to have the peace you see on these two young men?" I asked.

He said, "Yes," and we prayed together as he received the Lord.

Over the next couple of hours, this same scene repeated itself over and over. The fish were just jumping into the boat. I had done nothing to precipitate it; I was just receiving it.

When I looked around to see what the rest of the team was doing, I found them all praying with other people. The most amazing thing about this was that Jim was the only other one in the group who spoke any Spanish. The rest were ministering to people without even being able to communicate with them in the normal way.

It was now midnight, and I started heading for the hotel, but there was a small crowd still following me as I walked away. I told them that they could come to the Lord on their own if they liked, explained to them what kind of church they should look for and answered a few last-minute questions.

It wasn't until after we had all gotten back to our room that we began to realize the magnitude of what had just taken place. Each one of us had his own stories to share, and they were all truly amazing. As I listened to some of the others, the Lord spoke to me to get ready to see this phenomenon break out everywhere. This next harvest will be like nothing we have ever seen before. God is ready to use the weak, the small and the foolish — just as He always has.

CHAPTER 8

THE PEOPLE WHO KNOW THEIR GOD

But the people who know their God shall be strong, and carry out great exploits.

Daniel 11:32

I have already sprinkled several good stories of the miracles and wonders that I've seen in the last few years into the preceding chapters. Now, before I proceed to tell you more amazing stories of God's greatness, I must explain to you just how ordinary I really am. This is important so that no one will erroneously consider me to be just another "gifted man of God." If that happened, you might be able to disqualify yourself as being capable of moving in this same kind of favor from Heaven.

I was born on June 1, 1959, in Lima, Peru. As I have said, my parents were missionaries there, and so it was that I grew up on the mission field. If that sounds like an unfair advantage (spiritually speaking), I must point out that from the time I was four, our family was part of a very questionable movement. If I were to explain the full range of the doctrines and practices of the group, many would consider it to be a cult. (That story would require a whole other book.)

Those who know me marvel that I survived the period from four to eighteen years old. They were indeed trying times, for the group we were a part of was very spiritually abusive, and most of the kids my age eventually turned away from the Lord because of it. I was fortunate enough to become virtually "re-saved" at about the age of twenty, when I realized one day that I had grown up believing that righteousness was actually by works. I had never left the Lord, but there had been times when I was rather deceived about certain spiritual issues.

I continued to associate with this movement for years, until, at the age of twenty-seven, I became part of a great mega-church, and there I stayed for the next five years. One good part of that experience was that I met and married my wife Elizabeth while I was there. Elizabeth has been a great blessing to my life ever since. Together, we have had three beautiful daughters.

The negative part of the mega-church experience was that several of the main pastors of that church were discovered to be in various levels of adultery and other serious sins. Thus, we became embroiled in a highly-publicized scandal. (That story would fill another book.)

When this happened, we became so discouraged by the state of the church that we dropped out of doing "the church thing" for about three years. We still loved the Lord, but we weren't sure about many of His people. Then, in the mid-1990s, we began to hear about what people were calling the "Toronto Revival," or the "Toronto Blessing." I decided to go check it out in January of 1995. I went pretty much as a skeptic, wondering what, if anything, was in this latest wind of doctrine that the Charismatics had grabbed hold of.

Hank Haanegraaf, the now-famous church critic and watchdog, had become my hero, and I had come to believe that the problem with Christians was that they were too stupid and gullible. I firmly believed that the lack of "Christian intellect" was our greatest downfall. So many of the Christians who moved in power were so "screwed up" that I decided that the power itself must be "screwed up." Adding power to "this church thing" just seemed to complicate things. I went to Toronto with a chip on my shoulder, ready to critique what was now being called "the next Azusa Street Revival."

There were other feelings in me, however. Before I arrived in Toronto, I had also begun to hope that this new move was not a fraud at all. I knew that we needed something more.

My first night in Toronto was a momentous one. I didn't fall or shake, as many did, but as I was being prayed for at the close of the service, I wept for about an hour and a half, as I was deeply touched by the Holy Spirit. That experience changed my life forever.

It was interesting: The person praying over me that night prayed all the wrong things, but the more he prayed, the more I cried. This made him think he was on the right track, when he was actually not close at all. Still, the Lord used him as he was obediently doing his best. For it was the Lord Himself who ministered to me.

What changed forever that day was my perspective of God. In my worldview, God had become very tiny. I had come to feel sorry for Him for having such a "screwed up" Church. I just knew that until He sent Great Tribulation, His Bride was hopeless. Suddenly, I had a totally new perspective on things. It came not so much by what I heard, but by what I saw.

I had never seen so much of the power of God in operation. It was incredible to me. At Toronto, I personally talked to people whose lives had been turned around instantly through an encounter with God's power and love. I heard so many dramatic testimonies in rapid fire order that my faith became ignited. I began to desire to carry this power to so many who needed it.

That is the shortened version of my life ... up to 1995. I have never had a visitation by the Lord or one of His angels. I cannot claim that any famous anointed man or woman of God has prayed for me and released greatness into my life. I have never been on a lengthy full fast, not even one that lasted three days. Although my natural father had always been a good spiritual example for me, all other spiritual authority figures in my life have been seriously flawed. I had none of the marks of greatness that people usually look for when searching for those whom God will use. To the contrary, I had a seriously flawed spiritual background, and I am still quite ordinary in so many ways.

My qualifications for ministry are that I love the Lord very much, and I desperately want to obey Him. I probably also have a gift of faith, for if the Lord says that I can do something, I actually believe that I can.

A few months after my experience in Toronto, the Lord led me to go back and visit Peru. This was strange for two reasons. I had promised Elizabeth that I had gotten "the missionary thing" out of my blood and never intended to do that again. I had also told her that no matter what else God called me to do, it would definitely not be preaching. I had never been able to stand in front of a crowd without my mind going blank. God would have to use me in some other capacity.

I returned to Peru for the first time in nineteen years (except for one very short visit fifteen years before), and I went there to preach. I have already recounted some of the great things God did in Chimbote on that first trip, but there were many other significant events. First, of course, it was a significant event that I was even going to be preaching. How that came about is quite a story:

I called Pastor Darwin, whom I knew through my parents. We hadn't spoken with each other for many years, and I told him that I was coming to the country to reestablish friendships, explaining that the Lord had recently rekindled in me a love for Peru. He told me that he was glad that I was finally coming back to the country of my birth.

Several days later, the Lord showed me that He was not sending me just to "reestablish friendships"; He wanted me to release the anointing He had recently imparted to me. He gave me the name of five cities in Peru and told me to take this anointing to them.

I called Pastor Darwin back and told him that I wanted to have some meetings while I was in the country. I mentioned the five cities (Chiclayo, Trujillo, Chimbote, Lima and Huanuco) and asked him if he had contacts in those cities. A bit surprised, Pastor Darwin asked, "Do you preach now?"

"Yes," I answered him, "I do." That might appear to some to be a lie, but God had spoken to me to preach, so, therefore, it was no lie.

Pastor Darwin was able to set up meetings in four of the cities, and I received an invitation from other quarters to Huanuco.

The first place I was to preach was in Lima, the city of my birth. My first meeting there was on a Sunday morning, the last day of a week-long pastors' seminar. It was a yearly event that brought anywhere from fifty to eighty pastors under Pastor Darwin into the capital from all over the country. I had been hoping that I could get "broken in" with a smaller group. That Sunday morning, the church was totally packed. There were some two hundred and fifty people there.

As I have said, I hadn't spoken Spanish enough through the years to preach fluently in it, and besides that, I wasn't even accustomed to preaching in English. I wrote out my sermon and read it off the paper, looking up only once or twice in the middle of it. Then I asked the pastors if they would like to come forward and receive a special anointing from the Lord. I told them that they had received some good teaching during the week, but the Lord wanted to send them back to their congregations with power.

As the ministers came forward, I told them that the Lord was about to manifest Himself in their natural bodies as they had never felt before. They had nothing to fear; what they were about to experience was the Holy Spirit. From this ministry time we were about to have, they would be able to take home healing and revival to their churches.

I had the pastors stand and hold out their hands to receive from the Holy Spirit. Then I just asked the Holy Spirit to come and ignite His pastors. Within five minutes, all fifty pastors were shaking, crying, jumping, laughing, falling or in some other way, demonstrating that they were being touched by the Holy Spirit. After this wave of the Holy Spirit hit the pastors, it then spread into the congregation, and many who were attending were healed, delivered and otherwise elevated in their relationship with the Lord that day.

Many of those pastors did, in fact, take back a new anointing to their churches. Two of the pastors came up to me a year later and told me that they had now carried this new anointing to five cities. They reported many healings, salvations, deliverances and restorations. A paralytic stood up and walked in one of those meetings and remains totally healed.

We had another powerful meeting that night in Lima, and then we went on to Chiclayo. The church in Chiclayo had never seen anything like what I told them was about to hit them. They all shook and wept (and a lot more) until two in the morning. The pastor's son was delivered from demons. His was among the many usual testimonies of healing and restoration.

After that one night in Chiclayo, we went on to the city of Trujillo for one meeting. Three hundred people were packed into the church waiting for us when we arrived. This church had had some exposure to renewal, but the main leaders had expressed grave doubt that it was of God. All the people spent a lot of time on the floor that night shaking under the presence of the Lord. Many testimonies came out of that night as well.

I prophesied that the Lord was going to send a spiritual healing and revival *El Niño* upon those people and that their church, situated in the middle of the desert, would be "taken by the River." Within a few months, this had been fulfilled literally. *El Niño* floods carried the church away, and they are only now rebuilding. In the meantime, the congregation has thrived in various home church settings. Sometimes the Lord allows the natural to reveal what He is doing in the Spirit.

It was then that we went to Chimbote for a memorable meeting, and our last stop was the city of Huanuco. There, the Holy Spirit moved more strongly than He had in the other places. One reason is that we were able to have several meetings there rather than just one, and the presence of God kept building nightly.

The Huanuco church had a Christian Missionary Alliance background, but they had recently come into a love for the work of the Holy Spirit. They had been praying and seeking and asking the Lord to ignite them. He did — from the first meeting on. Several people had to be carried out to taxies, some because they were "drunk in the Lord," and others, because they just hadn't "come to" yet.

At about nine that night, one young man began to shake under the power of the Holy Spirit while still seated on one of the benches. His mother excitedly told me that he had just received the Lord that night before the meeting. At about midnight, she asked me if I had any idea when her son might stop shaking. I just laughed and told her, "Whenever the Holy Spirit is done with him."

Many great things happened during our days in Huanuco. The church where we were ministering is the largest in the city and was just waiting to be ignited. Within a year and a half, that church had planted sixteen other churches around the country — all under the power of the Holy Spirit.

The Huanuco church already had the custom of sending their young people into the central park for public witnessing. Usually one or two people came to the Lord as a result of their efforts, and there was nothing wrong with that. One night, I asked for all those involved in evangelism to come up for prayer. I told them that the Holy Spirit was now going to work with them like never before, but that they must give Him a chance. Instead of figuring out how they could win over the minds of the lost, I asked them to create an atmosphere for the Holy Spirit and then invite Him to operate.

About two months later, I heard from these young people. They said that the very next time they went out to the park to witness, thirty-two people had come to the Lord. Many had fallen down under the Lord's presence while saying the sinner's prayer. And, from that time on, they never had less than twenty people coming to the Lord on any given occasion.

There were also those who resisted the movings of the Holy Spirit in Huanuco. They accused me of being occultic and of possessing "lying signs and wonders." Even the pastor's wife was not too sure about all that was happening. She told me that she had been having a very hard time with it all until I said, "many of you are about to receive a confirmation that you have a gift of healing." I told them that they would immediately feel numbness in their right arms. She was thinking *Oh, brother*, when suddenly her entire right arm went numb. From then on, she believed.

Another leader was so opposed to what was happening that he was furious. He felt that the church was being totally ruined by these meetings, and he wanted nothing to do with them. He told his wife that he would not go to the next one. She said that was fine, but she was going. In the end, he attended, too, but he came in quite late. During the ministry time, his right hand began to vibrate from side to side. When this happened, all his resistance was broken down. He began to weep and thank the Lord. As the night wore on, that hand continued to vibrate from side to side in a very unusual way. At some point, he decided that he didn't want to waste the experience, so he began to go around laying his shaking hand on everyone he could.

One young man who was dramatically touched by the Lord during our days in Huanuco was a former member and leader of the Shining Path guerrilla movement. He had even been involved in the torture and killing of Christians. Then he had fallen out of favor with the group. He was beaten, tied up and thrown into the river to drown. A Christian couple rescued him as he drifted down-river by them. He came to the Lord and had been serving God in that church ever since. The Lord touched him very powerfully during our meetings, and he spent hours on the floor shaking under the presence of the Holy Spirit. The Lord was continuing an inner healing in him, igniting him in his giftings and callings.

In one of our final services in Huanuco, we asked this young man to give a testimony about what the Lord had done for him while we were there. He tried to share, but as he began to talk, he started the rather violent shaking again and then fell to the floor — where he shook for the rest of the meeting. He is now a fearless evangelist and also a pastor.

A year later, I prayed for this man again, this time for an even greater evangelism anointing to be released to him. His feet began to burn, only a little at first, and then more and more. I had seen this happen before. Those who have a strong evangelistic calling often feel their feet getting hot as we pray for them. The Scriptures say:

> *How beautiful are the feet of those who preach the gospel of peace, Who bring glad tidings of good things!* Romans 10:15

After a while, this young man's feet became unbearably hot, and the power on him was literally too much . He asked us to stop praying for him because he could not take it anymore. Then he took off his shoes and socks and began to rub his feet frantically, groaning in pain all the while. The whole process lasted about forty-five minutes, and when it was done, he had an even increased anointing in the area of his gifting.

After our last meeting in Huanuco, we received a rather strange request. We were asked to go to the largest private school in town and pray for all the high school students. It was a school where all the "who's who" of the city sent their children, but it was not a Christian school. Because I was still not a gifted speaker and I didn't know what to write down as notes, I wondered how such a meeting would go.

There was another problem. I was told that we could have five or ten minutes with each classroom. Between sharing and praying, that wasn't much time for us. I wondered if the Holy Spirit would move this fast.

On Monday morning, the team was standing with me in our first high school classroom. We had no idea what exactly we were to do, but our faith level was high because of what we had been seeing in the meetings. There were about thirty students in the classroom that day, and we were introduced to them as "visitors from America who would like to pray with you."

When I stood up, the only thing I could think of to say was, "How many of you have heard of God? Raise your hands." Every hand went up.

Next, I asked, "How many of you know that God loves you?" Again, all the hands went up.

I went on. "God is not a theology, and He is not a religion. God is a real person who interacts with us here on Earth. His agent of interaction is the Holy Spirit. We are going to pray with you right now, and the Holy Spirit will visit you as a real person. Some of you know, in theory, that God loves you, but before we have finished praying, you will know in reality that He loves you. Are you ready for that to happen?" In response to that, I received some not-so-sure nods.

I asked all the students to stand in front of their desks, hold their hands out and close their eyes. I then asked the Holy Spirit to visit them personally. Suddenly, tears began to gently roll down from many of their eyes. Then several students fell gently back into their seats. A few hands began to shake. At this point, because of the limited time, we began to lay hands on everyone in the room.

When we had accomplished that, I interrupted the process to say that we would be moving on now to other classes. I wish we had been able somehow to capture on video the looks on the faces of those students. It was obvious that they had received a touch from Heaven.

Before we left the classroom, I asked everyone, "How many of you now know that God loves you." Every head nodded in response. I told them to never forget that day and assured them that God had a plan for their lives if they would only give their hearts fully to the Lord Jesus. Then, we left.

We went on to four other similar classroom situations, and the results were just as amazing. In the very last classroom we visited that morning, something odd happened. As the rest of the students were being visited by the Holy Spirit, two young ladies at the very back of the classroom were mocking. They pointed to the students falling back in their seats and snickered. Then they looked at those who were weeping and then snickered again.

I walked to the back where the two young ladies were standing, went to the first one and said to her, "Hold out your hands." She did it, but there was a disgusted look on her face, and she turned to snicker with her friend. I put my hands on her hands, and when I did, big tears began to pour down her face. She quickly wiped them away, but others took their place. Tears kept coming. I said to her, "See, that's what your classmates are experiencing. And God loves you, too. Don't ever forget this experience."

I then proceeded to her friend, and the exact same scene repeated itself. As soon as I touched her hands, tears began streaming from her eyes. We watched as the Lord melted down open hostility with His relentless love.

The many things the Lord did during that first trip back to Peru were mind boggling. I have only shared here some of the highlights. These events took place in the nine days from August 10 to 19, 1996. We went to five cities, taking seven airplane flights, three bus trips and untold taxi rides. I preached eight times during those nine days and was in a total of forty or more hours of church services. At thirty-seven, I saw more fruit from those nine days of my life than from the rest of it all put together. Until then, I had had no idea that the Holy Spirit could do so much through my life if I would just be obedient to Him. Now I knew, and there was no turning back.

In February of 1997, we made the first of many trips to the Dominican Republic. As usual, I took a small team with me. The connection for that trip was made through Stephanie (the wife of the man who is now my associate pastor). She had spent several years as a missionary in that country before they were married. She had been involved in the formative stages of a small church that later mushroomed into the largest evangelical church in the country. While there, Stephanie had lived several years with a Dominican couple, Pastors Rafael and Rocio, and their children, and her relationship to them was still strong. She had told them of the trips we were taking and what the Lord was doing.

Although Pastor Rafael's church had experienced phenomenal recent growth, it had all happened through very hard work. He and other leaders of his church (about a hundred of them in all) had begun using a popular, U.S. based, church-growth plan. It had worked in that there were about five hundred new members attending the church, but the leaders had become little more than slaves to the situation, constantly responding to one crisis after another. They had become physically exhausted and spiritually dried up, and they were eager for relief. They had been fasting and praying for revival and an outpouring of the Holy Spirit.

By the time we arrived at the church, several other vessels of the Lord had passed through, trying to bring the presence of the Lord into the congregation. "We have everything but the power," Pastor Rafael commented to Stephanie. This, of course, is similar to having a marriage that has everything but love.

The idea of us going to bring revival to this church was really pretty silly. At the time, my team and I were not even related to a local church ourselves. We had neither a church home nor a ministry name. I was the only speaker in the group, and I have already told how limited my experience was at the time. We were going to a church that was very sophisticated in many ways. They were on national television and on radio, and they had some famous Dominicans among their membership. Rafael, Rocio and the other leaders were sincere, loving people with humble hearts and a desire to serve. The problem was that many good activities had squeezed out the activity of God.

Since I began traveling and ministering for the Lord, He has been very good to give me unusual confirmations that showed that He was with us. This trip was to be no different in this respect. The day we arrived in the Dominican Republic, it rained very hard. That would not seem to be unusual for that country, but according to the local people, it had not rained for nearly two months.

That first afternoon, before service, I was asked to pray for the pastor's father-in-law, as he was not well enough to go to the church. David (Stephanie's husband) and Mickey (an attorney from Chicago who has accompanied us on several trips) were with me, but I was the only one in the group who spoke Spanish, so I began praying over the man. As I was praying, I heard the distant roll of thunder. I wasn't sure why, but the next thing out of my mouth was, "Yes, Lord, send Your lightning against this sickness." Instantly, a bolt of lightening struck nearby, blowing out the power in the house and frying the backup battery that was kept for such occasions.

Mickey and David asked me, "What did you pray?"

"I asked for God to strike the sickness with lightening," I said.

I hadn't meant it in that way, I assured them, but the Lord was apparently giving me authority to have what I spoke. That fact greatly increased my faith. I never had the opportunity to ask the pastor's father-in-law when exactly he began to feel better, but he was in the meetings before we left.

Then as we walked into the church that first night, there was a "poof," and all the lights went out. It was not raining at the moment, and there was no lightening. I didn't feel any particular anointing, but the Lord was just showing us that He was with us. Since that time, the electricity has been affected in several places that we have gone, and it's a sign that His power is with us.

We don't have any control over this phenomenon. If we tried to show off an anointing by having electricity short-circuited wherever we went, it would never happen. And it may never happen again. But, then, it might. I've had microphones go out the minute I spoke my first word. When it happened, I just said, "Power, come back," and we were immediately back on again.

That first night in the Dominican Republic, the Holy Spirit did in fact "show up." Some of the pastors told me later that they had been feeling sorry for me. As I spoke and told them how the Lord was going to touch them at the end of the meeting, they doubted that it would happen. They were thinking, *It's too bad he doesn't know that the power and presence of God don't show up here. Yes, we want it. Yes, we repeatedly ask for it. Yes, ministers repeatedly tell us that we're going to experience it. Still, it just doesn't happen here. It's too bad. He seems like a nice enough guy.*

As another sign to this church that they were to heed our words, the Lord allowed us to bring a breakthrough fire to the people, much as it happened on our trip to Peru. The church has never been the same since.

As also happened in Peru, some were offended by this new move of God and eventually left the church because of it. However, new people came to the church to replace them. As a result, the church is breaking into full revival. It will be fun to see in the future what all the Lord does with them. They have already begun to plant other new churches and to send out missionaries. Some of their people have accompanied me on other ministerial trips and have been a great blessing.

Another sign that made us wonder occurred on this first trip to the Dominican Republic. We were sitting and talking with the pastor around his sturdy glass table. He was telling us what a blessing our visit had been, how he appreciated our down-to-earth, low-key presentation, and how the Lord had moved powerfully. I told him that I felt the Lord was just showing him an easier way to do His work. The Holy Spirit desires to carry the load for us — if we can just learn to lean on Him. He was bringing forth a new way of doing ministry, and being in the rest of the Holy Spirit.

As we spoke back and forth with each other in this way, there was a sudden loud bang. The thick glass table we were sitting around split down the middle, and nobody was leaning on it. The Lord was confirming the fact that He did have a new way He wanted things to be done. The old way of serving was to be over, just as that old table could no longer serve its purpose.

There was yet another sign that we experienced on that trip. A Toyota minivan came by to pick us up for church. The driver turned off the ignition and opened the doors so that we could get in. After we were all in, he proceeded to try to start the vehicle again. He turned the key repeatedly, but there was nothing but a "click." He started to get out to open the hood, but I said, "Just a minute!" I put my hands on the sidewalls of the van and said, "Power!" He tried it again, and the van started right up. I was as surprised as everybody else.

Faith often operates in this way, in quick reflexive acts, before faith-killing brain waves have time to react. This was also a case in which the anointing that was on us as a team had short-circuited the van. We apparently had the authority to get it back.

There were literally hundreds of people healed, delivered, ignited and otherwise touched by the Holy Spirit during our time in the Dominican Republic.

I suppose the greatest sign of God's favor on our efforts in the Dominican Republic occurred over a period of months. We returned with another team to the island four months later. After that first miraculous rain, it had rained daily during our visit, but then the rains had ceased again. As we flew over the land on our second visit, we noticed that all the vegetation had turned brown. We didn't know it at the time, but the island had not received a single drop of rain since we had left. The rains that fell during our first visit, four months earlier, had been the only relief in six months. Now, as our plane descended and prepared to land, I saw a rain cloud forming outside my window, and at the exact moment our wheels touched the runway, the rain burst from the clouds upon the land.

As we drove into town that day, children were out running naked in the rain, and adults were busy collecting water in anything they could. It rained every day while we were in the country. Eventually, it occurred to us to proclaim an end to the drought, and it was so.

We still wonder at this phenomenon. Why would the rain fall on the country only when we were there? We accepted it as a sign of God's favor.

On another trip, we experienced a violent earthquake after a powerful intercessory meeting in Trujillo, Peru. Although everyone there felt it, it didn't register at all on the Richter Scale. A volcano erupted the day we arrived in Costa Rica and made the front page of the newspapers. There was also some "unusual volcanic activity" the day we arrived in Nicaragua. When I was in Tocoa, Honduras, in 1999, the rest of Central America was being deluged with heavy rains. We rejoiced in a full week of dry weather in Tocoa. The satellite picture showed one giant swirl of cloud over all of Central America, with the exception of one small hole just over the Tocoa area. On another occasion, our arrival in Costa Rica spelled the end of six weeks of drought. And these unusual phenomena go on and on. It has become unusual for weather *not* to be affected by our visits.

None of these events are related to praying for something and having it happen. These things simply occurred when we went somewhere. There is an anointing that the Lord sends with us when we go in obedience to Him, and it just accomplishes things on its own. It doesn't matter if we don't have a chance to say a single word or to pray a formal prayer, the Lord still "does His stuff" anyway.

When we flew into Iquitos, Peru, the pastor and other leaders who met us at the airport told us later that when our airplane landed, they sensed "the strongest presence of the Lord they had ever felt." They had begun to weep. We had not even met them yet, but God had told them to receive what we were bringing. Our God is awesome.

The message I desperately want to convey through this book is that you may already have the power that you are waiting around for God to give you. How do you know if you have a healing anointing unless you start to pray for sick people? How do you know that God is not honoring your prayers unless you begin to do what you are praying for? I am convinced that if we would each begin to obey the simple things the Spirit tells us to do, there would be fruit from all of our lives.

Some may think that I went about the ministry all wrong. "Wouldn't it have been better to learn to preach first?" they might ask. I don't think so. If I had learned to preach first, I would have had something to lean on, and I would not have required the intervention of the Holy Spirit. When I launched out into Peru to preach, I had nothing to lean on but the Holy Spirit. He was enough, and He continues to be enough for my life and ministry today.

The purpose of this book is to reach out to those who are under bondage to false concepts. Just as Jesus instructed His disciples to untie the donkey He had need of, He is still looking for donkeys who are tied and need to be loosed. This book is not for the self-confident and self-satisfied. God cannot help the ambitious, the self-promoting, the proud and the unteachable. They will attempt great things in their own strength and will eventually fall on their faces.

There is an element of pride in the Body of Christ that has no place in what God is doing today. Many Christians believe that they are special, called, anointed and that they have risen above the average believer. This group is in great danger. If they are not careful, they will lose the baton, and it will be given to those who have *"no confidence in the flesh."* God is able to quickly bring into the Church former criminals, prostitutes and drug addicts, the uneducated, the rejected, the dispossessed and the battered and to release unbelievable power and glory through them. If you happen to be part of any of these groups and have only recently come to the Lord, get excited. If you will give your all to the Lord and learn of Him, there is no limit to how much God can use you.

If you are broken and have no confidence in yourself, you are God's vessel of choice. He uses fancy horses only when He cannot find enough insignificant donkeys. The glory of the last days will be poured out upon the humble and lowly. The fancy horses will be humbled or destroyed, for God will not share His Glory with those who exalt themselves. Vessels of pride may deceive many people for a season, but we know that they will not share in the glory of the last days. This is a different time. It is Triumphal Entry time, and glory thieves will be excluded from service to the Master. But the people who know their God and are humbly obedient will be used to achieve great things for His Kingdom.

CHAPTER 9

BEHOLD, I DO A NEW THING

Behold, I will do a new thing,
Now it shall spring forth;
Shall you not know it?   Isaiah 43:19

God is doing creative things these days, just as He did *"in the beginning"* of time. You don't have to try to copy what I have experienced. If each of us would step out in the creativity that the Holy Spirit wishes, there would be much more power released in our lives and ministries.

Many have no faith that God will move unless they use some existing model of ministry. Often this is just an unwillingness on their part to look foolish. The Holy Spirit can use almost any method to bring about the supernatural, and He loves variety. As we have seen, wonderful things can happen when we are willing just to blow a shofar, march or shout. There is no limit to what the Holy Spirit will use.

Let us seek new ways of serving the Lord. He loves it when we desire to do new things. If something we think of doing is not from Him, He is fully capable of putting a "check" within our spirits.

I want to share with you some of the unusual things we have seen just as examples.

THE INVISIBLE BOTTLE OF JOY

In Huancayo, Peru, at the end of one meeting, a young man walked up to me with a very sad look on his face. He asked me to pray for him to receive the joy of the Lord. He had many things warring against his joy, he said. I pretended to grab a bottle out of the air, I popped the cork, and then I poured the invisible bottle over his head. The noise in the meeting was very intense, and while I was doing all this, the young man had his eyes closed tightly, so I know he didn't see or hear what I was doing. Instantly, however, he was hit with some deep gut-wrenching laughter. He laughed for a very long time, until he was nearly in pain. He was rolling on the floor with laughter. The Holy Spirit released great joy into his spirit and loosed him from his heavyheartedness.

I could have ministered to him in the traditional way, but that creative thought just hit me, and I decided to go for it. I could not personally produce the joy he needed, and I knew that the Holy Spirit would not be offended by my lightheartedness. What happened was clearly a supernatural experience that deeply ministered to that young man.

Though we live in a very serious hour, we are called to live in this world with joy. The darker and darker the hour grows, the more we will need to find and walk in the joy of the Lord. If the joy of the Lord is our strength, then we will be weak without it.

THE ANOINTED GLOVES

While we were at that same conference in Huancayo, I saw something I had never seen before. In the middle of our ministry time, my brother-in-law Dennis (who is also a pastor) was helping to pray for people. Although we had a good number on our team, there were so many to pray for that we were all busy.

Huancayo sits at an altitude of eleven thousand feet in the Andes, and it was so cold that Dennis (like many others) was wearing gloves. At one point, he took off his gloves and laid one of them on one person's head and the other on another person's head. Meanwhile, he had his hands on two other people and was ministering to them.

It was interesting to see the two people with the gloves laying on their heads begin to shake under the power of the Lord released through those gloves. Eventually, they both fell in the Spirit. Then Dennis took the gloves and placed them on two more people, and the scene was repeated. It seemed to me that more power was being released through the unmanned gloves than through our hands. God, indeed, *"has chosen the foolish things."* The Holy Spirit did not have to release power through that very unusual method of ministry, but He chose to do it anyway.

THE HEALING TUNNEL

Once in the Dominican Republic we were in the midst of a special healing meeting. Instead of using one of the traditional methods of ministering to the people, I felt led to use what I have come to call "a healing tunnel." We had ten members on our team on this particular occasion, and we had five stand on one side and five on the other, facing each other. Then I had them hold hands across the gap with their arms held as high as possible. This formed a tunnel, and we had those who were sick to get in line and walk slowly through that tunnel.

Before the people started going through the tunnel, we asked the Holy Spirit to come and fill the tunnel and release healing on all who passed through it. I told the people that after they had gone through the tunnel, they were to return to their seats. If they found that their symptoms were gone, they could come forward and form another line, a testimony line.

That particular day, the Holy Spirit anointed the tunnel, and it was hard for people to get through it. Partway through, they would begin to stagger under the power of the Holy Spirit. Some had to be carried out after being overpowered by the Lord. Many fell down before they even got to the entrance of the tunnel, because such great power was being released through it. The line was moving so slowly that before we were halfway through the tunnel, there were at least fifteen in the testimony line who had been healed of every type of sickness and pain.

The greatest testimony I heard that day came from a woman who had been in the final stages of cancer. She felt the Lord's power flood through her body, and she knew she had been healed. Later that week, she went to her doctor, and he confirmed her total healing.

The following Sunday, the entire church service was taken up with testimonies of healing. Scores of people had been healed as they went through the healing tunnel.

During that healing service, we laughed a lot, we shouted a lot, and often the proceedings may not have seemed very orderly. People sometimes fell against the team members forming the tunnel, and they were toppled to the floor. There was a constant flurry of activity and readjustment, as people had to be carried to some other location. If you had walked into that meeting, it might not have seemed very orderly, as we may define order. In fact, the people might have seemed drunken.

Some, of course, might have thought that God was embarrassed by "all this foolishness" being done in His name, but they would have missed out on an encounter with the God of the Universe. They would have missed the healing of the cancer victim and the other scores of miracles that happened that day.

Some very good Christians would even call what we do, "lying signs and wonders." If God doesn't heal in a "dignified manner," they cannot accept it. Most people like that never see a healing miracle. They need to repent of the sophistication that separates them from experiencing God's supernatural power. Those who feel that it is their duty to warn the Church of "lying signs and wonders" need to at least be able to give examples of true signs and wonders. There cannot be a lying sign and wonder without a true sign and wonder. I will address this more fully in another chapter.

THE "HUMAN" RIVER OF GOD'S LOVE

Something unusual happened during our New Year's Eve service at the beginning of the year 2000. After worshiping with a song that spoke of "getting into the river," I felt that the Lord was saying that we needed to actually do it.

The River speaks of the flow of the Holy Spirit. In this River is everything that we have need of: healing, provision, direction and more. It's not a river of theology, but a River of God's presence.

Sound doctrine is important, but it only brings us to the banks of the River. It may point us to the source of the River, but at some point we must experience the River itself. God wants to make real to us His presence in the River.

If we choose to yield to His River and get into it, then we must surrender all control to the flow of the River. When we insist on retaining control, we have no choice but to remain on the banks of the River. Those who plunge in put themselves at the mercy of the River.

To some, it is risky to jump into the River; there is no way of knowing in advance where the River will take us. We may end up looking very foolish. Many "uncool" emotions may be evoked in the flow of the River. You might cry uncontrollably, laugh uncontrollably or shake uncontrollably. You might even be rendered immobile.

Many people want the benefits of the River without getting into it, but it just doesn't work that way. *"He has chosen the foolish things ...to confound the wise."* Don't be so *"wise"* that you miss the benefits of God's presence. Remember, *"In His presence is fullness of joy"* (Psalm 16:11).

Information about God is not the same as His presence. You can know the Bible by memory from cover to cover and still not experience His presence. To get into His presence, you must risk everything: your pride, your control, your dignity and your image. When you get desperate enough for God, none of these things will matter. You must somehow find your Source, and all our fountains are in Him.

We had the church people line up in two lines representing the borders of the river, and then we had them, one at a time, go through the River.

In several ways, I felt that this was a proper visual of what the Lord wants of us. We are called to be "channels" of the River. We can direct where it flows by where we go and let Him flow through us in that place. He rarely intervenes independent of His people. Since He is the Head, He releases His power through His Body.

As the people went through the River, it was as if God actually released a river of His presence. Many were actually pushed down upon their faces by the force of the water. They found themselves flat on their stomachs trying to crawl through the river but barely able to move.

In some ways, it was comical. If someone had come into the church in that moment, it would have looked like people were trying to swim on our carpet. No dignified Christian would ever want to look that foolish, but some of us desperate Christians are different. Nothing else satisfies us. The escapes provided by this world have left us hollow, and every Christian badge of prestige has become just as hollow. We desperately long to experientially connect with our Source.

Desperate people were touched by the Lord in many ways that night. Many said it was the most powerful encounter they had ever had with God. The fruit of it was an obvious increase of hunger and passion for the Lord in the lives of those who were touched.

I myself had no physical manifestation when I walked through the River. Of course, the people didn't really give me a chance. Many of the men picked me up and cradled me like a baby. At one point, they lifted me up over their heads as they shouted and prayed many things over me. Then they poured a whole bottle of oil on my hair. The oil ruined my shirt and left me with a matted head, but I must say that I did feel God's power, and my spirit was refreshed.

This happened at midnight, and the meeting went on until 6:00 a.m. the next morning. To some, I suppose, this must seem as utter madness, but I must say that our entire church has been at a different level since that night.

God is taking us to new levels, and this means greater authority over demons and disease. It means stepping into supernatural provision. It means being accompanied by more of God's presence wherever we go. It means an increase of vision and compassion.

"Could all this really be released in one night?" you might ask. Absolutely. Later, we may have to secure what we have taken in the Spirit realm and enforce our new boundary by evicting any hostile spiritual stragglers, but the victory can come in one night of obedient foolishness. While we take daily, inch-by-inch strides in our Christian walk, we must eagerly seek and recognize the opportunities the Lord gives us to make major gains in a single night of "foolish" experiences.

Unusual Healings

I have become so accustomed to seeing miracles that I am shocked when I see other Christians who are shocked that miracles haven't ceased. I sometimes recount healing miracles that I've seen, and I can sense that most of those who are listening to me are really struggling to believe it happened. These people know me well enough now to know that I wouldn't lie, but they still find the miracles to be unbelievable — based on their own experience. For these people, unbelief shows up as a refusal to really consider what I'm testifying of. They just go into "shutdown mode." I challenge *you*, the reader, not to do that. Ask yourself the following question: "Do I believe these reports?" If you don't, honestly ask yourself why you don't. One of the best ways to get rid of unbelief is to confess it. Do that and then step into the supernatural.

The Blind Man in Lima

One night in Lima, Peru, at the close of a service, I told the people that I wanted to ask each person specifically what he or she wanted prayer for, and then we would pray for that specific need. Nearly everyone we prayed for had a powerful encounter with the Holy Spirit. There were many reports of people being touched and healed by the Lord from that particular meeting.

In the middle of it all, I looked up and saw an elderly man with a cane being directed my way. He was obviously blind, and when I looked closer, I saw that both of his eyes looked milky, or cloudy. When it came his turn for prayer, I asked what he would like prayer for. Something in me was hoping that perhaps he was coming for some other need. "My eyes," he answered, confirming the obvious. I asked him if he was totally blind, or if could he see some. He answered that he was totally blind, but that he could see a bit of light out of his right eye, and he pointed toward the light in the room. No figures were discernible, he said, just a faint light, and to see that, he had to look directly at a light source.

I anointed the man with oil and asked the Lord to release His power on those eyes. As I did this, the man's eyes began to rapidly blink and tear up. This went on for a few minutes, and the man became very animated. I asked him to tell me what was happening. Nearly hyperventilating, he said, "I can see more light in this eye," and he pointed to his right eye. I told him to continue looking at the light. There were many others to pray for. I promised to return in a few minutes to see how he was.

When I came back to him a few minutes later, I saw him looking at the palm of his hands. I asked him, "Can you see your hands?" Now he was even more excited, and he nodded that he could.

I let out a little shout of "All right!" and then asked him, "What about your other eye?" He closed his now-seeing eye and looked with the other one. Then he shook his head, indicating that he still saw nothing with that eye. I told him that I felt that I should anoint him again with oil and keep speaking to both eyes, and I did. I spoke to the eyes, commanding them to "come back, in the name of Jesus." I spoke to the cloudiness and commanded it to leave.

During this entire time, there was a visible manifestation of God's power on the man, and the seeing eye kept getting progressively better. This was encouraging because when one eye has already been healed, that has a way of igniting faith for the other eye.

I told the man that I would be back, and again, I went off to pray for others. When I came back this time, he said, "I can see light in my other eye now." This ignited even more faith. I continued praying with him for several minutes until he was able to see his hands clearly — and mine. I then had to leave him and continue praying for others.

By the end of the meeting, the work was done, and I was able to point him out to the congregation as a man who had come in blind but now could see. He confirmed it, from the fourth row where he was sitting. He could see both me and the writings and pictures on the wall behind me. When he left the meeting that night, he was twirling his cane over his head. This miracle opened up other wonderful ministry opportunities around the country, including a trip to Iquitos, deep in the jungles, where we were able to minister to several churches and their pastors.

An Elderly Man With a Fractured Wrist

In Huanuco, Peru, an elderly man came forward for prayer. I asked him what he needed, and he showed me his wrist. It was apparent that there was something seriously wrong with it, as it had a large knot on it. He said that he had fallen and fractured his wrist some time before, and that he hadn't been able to afford to have it "fixed." I took his hand and began to ask the Lord to send His power to heal the man. Then, I began speaking to the bones in his wrist, telling them to go back into place. The Lord's power came on the man, he began to weep, and his hand and wrist began to shake.

When this intensified, it frightened the man. He felt a great heat in his wrist, and it flowed all the way up to his elbow. It was becoming stronger. I told him not to be afraid, that this was the Lord healing him.

Suddenly, while we were all watching, the bones began to move under the skin. They were being pushed back into place. Then, just as suddenly as it had begun, it was completed.

As is often the case in countries like Peru, we had no before and after x-rays to confirm exactly what the problem had been and what God had done, but we could all see the difference. The wrist now had a totally different appearance. The knot was gone, and the man knew that he had been healed.

THE MAN WITH THE FAT FINGER

Right after we prayed for the man with the fractured wrist, another man came up and showed me his middle finger. It was at least twice the normal thickness. He said that an injury suffered years before had left his finger in this condition.

I prayed, asking for the Lord's power to come into that finger. It came with such suddenness and power that the man grabbed his finger and began rubbing it. It had gotten very hot, and he, too, was concerned about what was happening. When the heat and power were finally bearable, he let go of the finger, and we could all see that it had returned to its normal size. The whole process had taken about five minutes, but the miracle was evident for everyone to see.

THE MAN WITH ABDOMINAL PAINS

Later, in that same meeting, another man came forward. He pointed toward his lower abdomen and told me that he'd been having problems in that area of his body for years. He had undergone surgery to see if anything could be done, but the pains had continued.

I asked the Lord to release His power to that man. Suddenly, he looked up at me and said, "It's all better!"

"What do you mean?" I asked.

He said, "The pain just left, and I can tell I'm totally healed!" He started jumping around to show us that he really meant it.

THE LITTLE GIRL WITH A HIGH FEVER

In Tocoa, Honduras, I was asked to go to a home and pray for a four-year-old girl who was very sick. When I was taken inside, I saw her lying in a deep sleep on a very dirty sofa. Her mother had died suddenly some two months before, and it was apparent that her father was struggling to keep the household running. The girl had accidentally cut herself while working with a machete, and her wound had now produced a serious infection. Her body was fighting the infection with a high fever.

I went near to the child and felt her forehead. What I felt was alarming. We have three small daughters ourselves, and I knew from the touch that this was a very dangerous fever. I had never felt anything like it before. Her whole body seemed to be "on fire." The child did not even stir.

The first thing that came to my mind was to ask if there was any medicine to give her, but then I remembered that they had brought me there to pray for a miracle. I left my hand where it was on her head and began to command the fever to leave. Within a couple of minutes, the fever had gone out, and her forehead felt cool under my hand.

I called the father over and had him feel his daughter's head. He agreed that the fever was gone. That night I asked about the child and was told that she was completely healed.

As I left the house that day after prayer, I hugged all the members of the family one by one, as is customary. As I hugged another of the daughters, I noticed that she too had a burning fever. I asked her if she was sick, and she answered that she had malaria. They had been so concerned about the smaller sister that malaria hadn't seemed serious enough to seek prayer for. I prayed for her, too, keeping my hand on her head for a good while. For some reason, her fever did not seem to go down right then. That night, however, they told us that the fever had broken after we left the house and that her malaria was gone. Why did one fever go immediately and one take a couple of hours? I don't know. I'm just glad that they both went.

MANY, MANY MORE

I could go on and on with stories like these. They bring me great joy to remember them. In our services, people are being delivered of demons and healed of every type of sickness, disease and injury, including back pains, breathing problems, ulcers, panic attacks, cancers, lupus, blindness, high blood pressure, stomach ailments, migraine headaches, allergies, colds, fevers and every other kind of "aches and pains." Hundreds of healings like these have occurred since 1996, and I am expecting the number to increase exponentially.

This all happened, not because I am someone great or someone especially anointed, but because I am ordinary and know that I can do nothing without Him. I trust that these testimonies will free you to begin to perform the works the Lord has stored up for you to do. If He can do such things through me, He can surely do them through you, too. How do you know there are not great things that you could be doing right now? Are you waiting for somebody to tell you that you are anointed before you begin? Do you need man's approval first? Does somebody need to recognize that you are doing important ministry before you can become active?

There is an army of intercessors at work in the world, and its members often receive little recognition. They are much more responsible for the recent gains the Body of Christ is making than are those who are more visible. As I go from church to church, the Lord often shows me individuals who are the real lifeline of a particular ministry. It is often not the pastor — unless he is also a true intercessor.

True intercessors are God's frontline warriors today. Many of them are not able to share their stories and prove that God is with them, yet they do what they do obediently and often with no human acknowledgment or encouragement. The Lord Himself is their reward. One day they will receive full credit for what they have done. They are truly a 1 Corinthians 1:25-29 company. They are often subject to ridicule for the foolish way they are gripped by the burden of intercessory prayer. They are constantly overlooked, under-appreciated and often beat up by Satan. If the Lord has called you into the ministry of intercession, don't underestimate its value. The more need you have for people to know about you, the less authority will be given to you. Sometimes we have a choice — to be known on Earth or to be known in Heaven.

This is an area where almost anyone of us can begin a ministry. If you have been squelched in every other way by so-called church politics, this is a good field to get started in. No man can stop you in this area. You also don't have to wait to receive a prophecy telling you that this is your calling. Jesus, the Head of the Church, sits at the right hand of the Father and lives in constant intercession for us (see Romans 8:34 and Hebrews 7:25). We, as His body, should do as the Head does. Everyone can have the ministry of intercession.

There are many other ways to be activated into ministry. The whole world is our arena of responsibility. There are needy people everywhere: in hospitals, jails, nursing homes, orphanages, parks and malls. If you can settle for being known only in Heaven, there is great opportunity awaiting you. If you require some of the glory for yourself, this great end-time outpouring may pass you by. God is searching for donkeys who will respond obediently to His creative and powerful direction.

CHAPTER 10

—————

THE EARNEST PRAYER OF
A RIGHTEOUS MAN

The earnest prayer of a righteous man has great power and wonderful results. Elijah was as completely human as we are, and yet when he prayed earnestly that no rain would fall, none fell for the next three and one half years! Then he prayed again, this time that it would rain, and down it poured and the grass turned green and the gardens began to grow again.

James 5:16-18, TLB

Most people know who Sammy Sosa is. He, along with Mark McGwire, stunned the baseball world in the late 1990s by breaking the home run records of Babe Ruth and Roger Maris. What has made Sammy Sosa stand out is the amazing power he has displayed in a five-foot-ten-inch frame. Mark McGwire is an imposing six-foot-five-inch man who has taken some questionable vitamin supplements. This is not to take anything away from him (for what he has done is truly amazing), but it does further accentuate Sammy's accomplishments.

When I teach on healing these days, I teach what I have come to call "the Sammy Sosa Principle." The game of baseball has many truths that can be applied to praying for the sick. The stories I have told here and others like them could be compared to a blow-by-blow descrip-tion of the sixty-six home runs that Sammy Sosa hit in 1998. If you watched the video highlights that year, you got the feeling that he was hitting a home run virtually every time he got up to bat. This, however, was not even close to the truth.

Sammy Sosa had some six hundred plate appearances that year, and he hit sixty-six home runs. That means that nearly nine out of every ten times he came to the plate, he *did not* hit a home run. In fact, in 1999, Sammy Sosa struck out more than any other player in Major League Baseball. Only real baseball fanatics know these facts.

Still, Sammy Sosa is paid some ten million dollars a year by the Chicago Cubs, and he receives millions more for his appearances in commercials. Why is Sammy Sosa paid millions of dollars for failing nine times out of ten? It's because his home run total over-shadows his failures. Sammy swings so hard that if he gets enough chances he will out-homer nearly everyone.

I learned a lot through watching Sammy Sosa go through that batting season. He went through stretches when he hit home runs almost every day, but he also went through long stretches when he struck out time after time. The interesting thing to me was that no matter how well or poorly Sammy did on a respective day, he did not change his swing. He might strike out ten times in a row, but on the eleventh time at bat, he would still swing just as hard as he could. He envisioned a home run at every at-bat, so he didn't soften his swing or use a lighter bat.

In his dry times, Sammy could have gone for some so-called blooper hits so that his critics would stop talking about the slump he was in. But no, Sammy Sosa just kept swinging hard at every ball that came his way. He knew that his swing was a good one. It had good plate coverage, and it had a history of good power. If he over-analyzed his swing after every strike-out and got depressed about all his misses, he would have spiraled down into discouragement and become a useless hitter.

Baseball is a sport where each player must focus on the positive. This is true for us in the healing ministry as well. Paul wrote to the Philippian believers:

> *Whatever things are of a good report, if there is any virtue and if there is anything praiseworthy — meditate on these things.*   Philippians 4:8

These are golden words for men and women in all walks of life.

In baseball, a given baseball player will always have more swings and misses than hits and home runs. Yet if he can keep from becoming discouraged and losing his confidence, he can still receive millions of dollars for what he does accomplish. The term "losing confidence" is the description given to a player who is in a terrible hitting slump. Announcers will hardly discuss his swing or the way he stands in the batter's box. They speak of his confidence. If a hitter is in a particularly good stretch, it will be said of him that he is "hitting with a lot of confidence" and vice-versa.

There are many lessons for us to learn from this. First, always swing hard — even if you strike out a lot. Every time I pray for a sick person, I "swing hard." Ten people in a row may not be healed through my prayers, but I still believe that the next one will be the one. Sometimes I may actually be losing confidence, but then the Lord gives me a home run that boosts my faith.

Hitting with confidence in baseball is equivalent to praying for the sick in faith. If you will keep doing it, results will begin to come.

The key to hitting many home runs is having many "at bats." Many Christians, when they have prayed for a few people and there were no results, have determined that they do not have a healing gift. That conclusion is as foolish as a baseball player giving up after three times at bat. Until you have had at least fifty "at bats," you can't know if you need to change your swing. In the same way, it is impossible to determine if you have a healing gift until you have prayed for a good number of people.

Just as in baseball, there are many ways to swing. Some swing right-handed; some swing left-handed; some stand in back of the batter's box; some stand in front of it; some have a funny-looking crouch; and others stand straight up. As long as you cover the plate with your swing and do so confidently, good things will happen regardless of what your batting stance happens to be.

The baseball term, "covering the plate," for the Christian could signify praying the right prayer. I believe that there are many "right" prayers, but some prayers just don't seem to accomplish much. Jesus used many different types of prayers, and men and women who have been used by God in this area of ministry have done the same.

For me, speaking to the problem at hand is the type of prayer that seems to release the most faith. If someone has a headache, I pray, "Headache, go away — in the name of Jesus." Sometimes I first ask the Lord to send His power upon the person, and then I speak to the problem.

The type of prayer that I have found to be least effective is what I would refer to as a "begging prayer." An example might be, "Oh Lord, You know about sister so-and-so. You know how she has served You all her life. You know how faithful she's been to You. Lord, she doesn't need this headache. Lord, she wants to be able to concentrate on serving You. Oh Lord, please heal her, etc., etc." Although this prayer may make the sick person feel loved and cared for, it seems to release very little healing faith or power.

Therefore, if a kidney needs healing, I address the kidney. If a bone is broken, I speak to the bone. If ligaments are the problem, I speak to them in Jesus' name. We are to exert the authority the Lord has given to us (see Luke 10:19).

One of the worst traits to have when ministering to the sick is "excessive thinking." This is also true in baseball. Brain waves are not channels for the Lord's power, and an excess of them invariably short-circuits faith. If you pray for the sick and are constantly warring in your mind, then you will short-circuit the operation of faith. In baseball, this is called a "check swing." Usually, all that a check-swing gets you is a foul ball.

As believers, we must know that we have been given authority to heal the sick, and we must believe that it is God's will for the sick to be healed. Questioning these two issues will always short-circuit the power of the Lord. To think otherwise is a theological "cop-out" designed to cover us when we swing and miss.

If we are constantly asking ourselves, "Do I have enough faith for this?" or "Does the sick person have enough faith for this?" or "Is there too much unbelief in this room?" or "What if nothing happens? What will I tell them?" we exhaust ourselves and lose faith. Swing hard every time — no matter what happens, and leave the results with God. If the Holy Spirit reveals some helpful information to you while you are praying, use it, but if not, just swing hard and keep swinging, and you will begin to hit some home runs.

At times, the Holy Spirit has showed me that there was some unforgiveness blocking healing in the person I was praying for, and I have had to minister to the person on that issue before healing would come. At other times, I may sense that something is blocking the healing, but I won't know what it is. In this case, I still swing hard. Until I receive some advanced gifting (perhaps equivalent to getting a new bat in baseball), I just have to swing hard with what I have. I know that I don't have an impressive array of gifts in this area, and I am constantly looking for the Holy Spirit to upgrade these gifts, but in the meantime, I am doing the best I can with what I have.

I can't see into people's bodies, as some do, and know precisely the problem and what the Lord is doing about it. I hope to receive this gift at some point. I don't feel specific virtue leaving my body that tells me a healing has taken place, as some do. That would be a good gift to have as well. The list of what I don't have is long, and I do have a petition before God for better tools. But I have still seen many successes already — due to the fact that I swing hard. Somehow I know that I just might hit the ball, and if I do, I want it to go far.

I suppose the ability to swing hard is a gift of faith, and I do thank the Lord for giving me that. It is the "Sammy Sosa Principle" that I use most. "Swing hard," I tell people, "because sooner or later you'll hit something." This principle actually applies to many other areas besides ministering healing, and we can apply it anywhere it fits.

When I go into any country, I pray the biggest prayers I can for that country and for the particular city I'm in at the time. I swing hard. I assume that the Lord wishes for revival to be released everywhere. I assume that He wishes multitudes to be saved everywhere. I assume that angels need to be released everywhere. I assume that

God has a great destiny for every city and every country, and I do my best to call it forth. I pray and proclaim anything and everything that the Holy Spirit doesn't restrict me from saying.

Can it hurt? The worst thing that can happen is a swing and a miss, but if that happens, I can always look forward to my next "at bat." Revival is being unleashed in many countries and cities because I and others like me dare to swing hard. God's Word declares: *"The earnest prayer of a righteous man has great power and wonderful results"* (TLB).

In the King James Version of the Bible, this phrase *"the earnest prayer"* is translated as *"the effectual fervent prayer."* This is not just a prayer; it is a very specific type of prayer. In baseball terms, it's the difference between "a swing" and "a hard swing." The original Greek word for the adjective that precedes the word "prayer" is *energo*. We might translate the combination of these two words as "the hard-swinging prayer."

In his day, Elijah surveyed the situation around him and correctly discerned that he needed a home run. He went up to the plate and swung with all his might. The Lord apparently ordered a fast ball right down the middle (those are the easiest ones to hit), and Elijah "nailed" it. It happened because he swung hard. He prayed an *"earnest prayer,* an *effectual fervent prayer."*

Many have incorrectly thought that the emphasis in James 5:16 is on the *"righteous man,"* and wondered if they were righteous enough to receive answers to their prayers. Verse 17 followed to make sure we didn't get the wrong message. It tells us that *"Elijah was as completely human as we are."* The King James Version says, *"Elias was a man subject to like passions as we are."* The Modern Language translation says, *"Elijah was a man of similar weaknesses with us."*

This passage is clearly not trying to distinguish the wonderful results that Elijah received (his home run) as being based on his righteousness. It is the *energeo* prayer that is the focus. No matter how much your "righteousness resume" grows, it cannot compete with standing in the righteousness of the Lord Jesus Christ. Isaiah warned us:

The Earnest Prayer of a Righteous Man

All our righteousness is as filthy rags.   Isaiah 64:6

The book of Romans shows us repetitively that righteousness is by and through faith in what Jesus did on the cross. As we appropriate His sacrifice, we are credited with righteousness (see particularly Romans 4:1-8). Good behavior is not righteousness; being covered by the Lord's work of atonement is righteousness.

Yielding to that work of atonement will eventually cause good behavior to become a by-product, but the behavior in itself cannot grant us righteousness. Many Christians are confused in this regard. Acceptable righteousness cannot have us as its source, because all our righteousness is *"as filthy rags."*

If we are clear on how to be considered righteous, we might be able to put a little more *energeo* into our prayers. The Greek word that is translated "prayer" here is *deesis*. It is not the word for "intercession," which is *entugchano*. *Deesis* means simply "prayer request or petition." This would be equivalent to a batter's swing. In intercession, we actually birth something in the Spirit. It's a process. But then there is also place for simple, quick, hard swings. I think that if we knew the truth, we would all be surprised at how many opportunities to hit home runs we have missed simply because we did not swing hard.

Recently, I had the choice of swinging hard or going for a weak blooper. Let me tell you about it.

THE LITTLE GIRL AND HER MEAN GRANDPA

In Tocoa, Honduras, a young lady came to us for prayer one morning. When she shared her prayer request, she began to weep. She was a single mother with a four-year-old daughter. For financial reasons, the two of them were forced to live with her parents. Her problem was that her father was still deeply angry with her for having a child out of wedlock, and he was taking his revenge by totally shunning the granddaughter. He had never been willing to show her any kindness. This mother's heart was broken, and she felt she could no longer bear to see her daughter go through the daily mistreatment and rejection.

This was a unique prayer situation. Obviously, the mother had some personal rejection that she, too, was working through. At the same time, she was feeling her daughter's pain, quite possibly more than her own. I found myself trying to determine just what I should pray for in this situation.

A "safe" prayer came to my mind. It was that the Lord minister to the pain the woman was feeling as a mother, and that the burden of her heart be lifted. There would have been nothing wrong with such a prayer, for it addressed actual needs. But, suddenly, I felt a need to swing hard. A much riskier prayer came to mind. If I prayed this prayer, I had a much higher chance of failing, but I felt I needed to "go for it."

I began to pray, asking the Lord for a miracle. I prayed, "Lord, we ask You to change Grandpa's heart. We ask You to change that heart of stone and make it a heart of flesh again. We ask for Your divine intervention ... ."

When the mother arrived home that day, her daughter ran to her and blurted out, "Something has changed Grandpa's heart," and she showed her mother a little gift her grandfather had given her. It was the first nice thing he had ever done for her. The mother shared all this with me that night in church, and as she did, she sobbed and sobbed.

The next night, Grandpa himself came to church, and during prayer time, he was significantly touched by the Lord. On our last day there, the young mother told me that miracles were increasing daily in their home and that she would write it all down and send it to me because it was so significant.

It is time for us to begin to pray some better prayers toward our unsaved family members. We risk disappointment, and we risk frustration, but we must stop thinking that way. We can never hit home runs if we are worried about striking out. If we get enough hard swings in, sooner or later the Lord will order a hitable pitch to be sent to us. Never forget, *"The [energeo] prayer of a righteous man has great power and wonderful results."*

God wants to bless us each with *"wonderful results,"* so let's give Him a chance to do it. Paul admonished:

> *But ye, brethren, be not weary in well doing.*
>
> 2 Thessalonians 3:13, KJV

The reason Paul felt compelled to give this counsel was that he knew that *"well doing"* does not always have quick rewards. As in baseball, we must settle in for the long haul, as we daily "go for it." When our focus turns to the swings and misses, weariness sets in. Keep your focus on your present "at bat" and the fact that you have another chance at hitting a home run. The Lord has promised:

> *And it shall come to pass in the last days, says God, that I will pour out of My Spirit on all flesh.*
>
> Acts 2:17

There is coming a last-days outpouring that will decidedly tip the scale in favor of those who are "swinging." Because of this outpouring, suddenly we will "kill" pitches that we have previously been unable to hit. The enemy will think we have been cheating and using illegal steroids and supplements because we will be doing so well. Those who keep swinging will receive power supplements. That, in itself, should keep us motivated to stay active. I trust that you can use the Sammy Sosa Principle in your everyday Christian life.

CHAPTER 11

LET US LAY ASIDE EVERY WEIGHT

Therefore we also, since we are surrounded by so great a cloud of witnesses, let us lay aside every weight, and the sin which so easily ensnares us, and let us run with endurance the race that is set before us. Hebrews 12:1

Just what holds you back? I have already offered several challenges to the readers, but I want to further challenge you with the words of the writer of Hebrews. Hopefully, by now you realize that there is more danger with being overqualified to receive God's anointing and power than there is from being underqualified. The more underqualified you appear to men, the more likely you are to be God's vessel of choice.

The writer begins this chapter by reminding us that we are *"surrounded by so great a cloud of witnesses."* In the previous chapter, he named many of those witnesses: Abel, Enoch, Noah, Abraham, Sarah, Isaac, Jacob, Joseph, Moses, Joshua, Rahab, Gideon, Barak, Samson, Jephthah, David and Samuel and other Old Testament heroes of faith. In the New Testament, we have many others — Mary, John the Baptist, Peter, James, John, Mary, Martha, Stephen etc. — who are also part of this *"cloud of witnesses."* The purpose of pondering these witnesses is to stir us to run the race as never before.

The writer uses the word *"since"* as an added incentive for us to press in. He was saying, "Since we are surrounded by these incredible servants of God," let us strive to equal their exploits.

In the eleventh chapter, we were told of the price many of these great men and women paid for their faith, and the writer is using that to challenge us. Their diligence and perseverance presents a powerful example for us all. From these who have gone before, we can receive, therefore, an impartation of motivation.

Apparently these men and women can watch what we are going through today. *The Living Bible* says it this way:

> *Since we have such a huge crowd of men of faith watching us from the grandstands, let us strip off anything that slows us down or holds us back, and especially those sins that wrap themselves so tightly around our feet and trip us up; and let us run with patience the particular race that God has set before us.*

When I read this, I get the picture of a large stadium, with all those who have gone before us as spectators in the stands. As they sit back and watch us run, we are motivated by the example they have left us.

Our first motivation, of course, is to please our Owner, but the spectators are also to be considered. We don't want the spectators booing us, even if it's the Owner who "cuts our checks." Those who are now in the stands were once on this very same playing field. In fact, they played in this very same contest. This has been a very long contest, and we are still strongly feeling the impact of what the former players have done.

The present spectators have earned some well-deserved heavenly rewards. Many of them were the only obedient voices in their generations, and their pioneering obedience is to be lauded. Most of them ran against an overwhelming tide and didn't have as many examples to learn from as we now have.

Let there be an impartation of motivation to your heart today through considering those who have gone before. Something in us should stir us to not want to disappoint them. Every time we use manipulation and self-promotion, it is not just the Lord who sees it and is saddened; the courageous men and women of God who went before us also see. Every time we sow discord, these spectators see it. Every time we lie, backbite, gossip or tear each other down in any other way, these spectators are watching. They are witnesses of how we run this race.

We must be motivated to lay aside every weight through remembering these great men and women of faith. They notice when we refuse credit we could be taking. They notice when we turn the other cheek — even when we feel like striking back. They see us in our closets weeping over our cities, our countries and our families. They see when we've been overlooked and we don't wrongfully respond. They take notice when we choose to trust again after we have been badly "burned" by someone.

There is a grandstand full of people whom we would not like to disappoint through our many excuses. They know what living in this world is all about. If we have difficulty imagining Jesus as fully human, we should definitely have no problem knowing that these men and women were. They certainly know the full pangs of every human temptation. The Bible states that Jesus was tempted in every way, just as we are (see Hebrews 4:15). If that is not easily understood (because He was also God), at least we must be challenged by the life of these witnesses who were not in any way divine.

Considering Jesus Christ and the incredible love of the Father should always be our first and greatest motivation, but the writer is recommending these witnesses as a further motivation. This will serve those who sometimes find themselves angry with God for some reason.

We cannot pray to these witnesses, and they apparently cannot pray for us, but somehow I believe they have the freedom to point us out. Something in me tells me that there is some value in this. If God is influenced by even our desires, then I believe He can also be influenced by their desires. How this all plays out is speculation on my part, but let us allow the awareness of the spectators to provoke us to righteousness. Let us "ditch" the excuses and the fears that make up most of "the weights" we are being encouraged to lay aside. Let us no longer allow sin to entangle our feet. Let us stop flirting with it and, instead, give our energy to "swinging hard" for our Lord.

I feel sure that this *"cloud of witnesses"* would love to talk to us. They now know God as He really is. They now know the unimaginable beauty and grandeur of Heaven. They can now taste the indescribable fullness of God's love. They now know the full *"width"* and *"length"* and *"depth"* and *"height"* of the love of God (Ephesians 3:18). I am fully convinced that the one regret we will all have when we stand with them one day is that we did not serve God more passionately and selflessly. When we stand with them, we will discover how incredibly awesome our God has been all along. These witnesses already know the fullness of this truth.

Even though the writer of Hebrews still only knew in part, he recognized the value of *"running with endurance."* Every Christian should prepare himself as a marathoner. Even if the Lord were to come tomorrow, we must develop a marathoner's mentality. Jesus said:

> *Blessings on you if I return and find you faithfully doing your work.*
> Matthew 24: 46, TLB

Though endless speculation about the end-time seems to be the full-time ministry of many today, the Lord will bestow "blessings" on those who are *"faithfully doing [their] work."* It may be much more fun to drop out of the race and concentrate on speculation about how it will all end, but don't get caught in that trap. You will be blessed if you remain in the arena of Christian service. The ministry of end-time speculation is not a legitimate one. As we grow nearer to the end, the Lord will begin to reveal to us more and more of His mysteries. But such revelations will come supernaturally through those who are *"faithfully doing [their] work,"* not to those who are standing idly on the sidelines.

God is giving us many road signs, indicators of what is to come. Intellectual studies of the Scriptures alone will not reveal the prophetic timetable of end-time events. The Pharisees had hundreds of years to study and interpret the Old Testament, and still they were deceived. Study did not help even one of them to recognize the very event for which they had been waiting. It was happening before their eyes, and they didn't know it. Only Anna and Simeon recognized the Christ, and they were among those who were *"faithfully doing [their] work."*

Matthew pointed out nine times in his gospel that something that had occurred was *"that what was spoken through the prophet might be fulfilled."* He referred to prophecies by Isaiah, Jeremiah, Hosea, David, Samuel, Zechariah and Daniel. How did Matthew recognize all these prophetic fulfillments, when the "prophecy experts" didn't understand even one of them? It was not through study. That's for sure. Matthew's background was tax-collecting, not eschatology. Prophecy experts are wrong about ninety-nine percent of the time. As we have seen, the natural mind cannot know things that must be spiritually discerned. True prophetic revelation will come from the belly (the innermost being) and not from the brain.

This is not to say that prophecy experts don't love God or that they are false brethren. I don't believe that is generally the case. The problem is that much of what is being touted as prophetic study is mere speculation.

What will the prophecy experts do when their predictions don't come true? Will they become like the Pharisees and reject what God is doing? Will they be willing to accept that which violates all their preconceived ideas? Will their influence cause many others to reject the unfolding of God's plan? I hope not.

It is unwise to follow or promote prophetic speculation. For one thing, it is a waste of valuable time. Also, if you get too attached to it, you may have difficulty letting go of it when it fails. No biblical prophet ever gained his information through research. Not one of the men Matthew mentioned prophesied Jesus' coming and His works through study. They moved totally in the spiritual realm. Jesus Himself said:

> *Watch therefore, for you know neither the day nor the hour wherein the Son of man is coming.*   Matthew 25:13

But of that day and hour no one knows, neither the angels in heaven, nor the Son, but only the Father.   Mark 13:32

If even the angels and Jesus Himself don't know the timing of these events, how can any human know it? Will God show something to a "biblical mathematician" when He hasn't even told Jesus about it? I think not.

Some prophecy experts claim to be following the instruction of Mark 13:33:

Take heed, watch and pray: for you do not know when the time is.
                                                            Mark 13:33

But what does it mean to *"watch"*? Does it mean that we should try to guess the timing of the upcoming events? No. We are simply to be ready so that when it happens, we won't be surprised.

Jesus went on:

It is like a man going to a far country, who left his house and gave authority to his servants, AND TO EACH HIS WORK [emphasis mine], and commanded the doorkeeper to watch. Watch therefore, for you do not know when the master of the house is coming — in the evening, at the midnight, at the crowing of the rooster, or in the morning — lest, coming suddenly, he find you sleeping. And what I say to you, I say to all: Watch!
                                                            Mark 13:34-37

The Lord has given each of us our *"work,"* and He hopes to find us *"faithfully doing"* it when He comes. Notice who He commanded to do the actual "watching." It was *"the doorkeeper."*

Who is *"the doorkeeper"*? He is clearly not one of the sheep, but the Holy Spirit Himself (see John 10:3). Therefore, when the Lord commands us to *"watch,"* He is not asking us to do the work of the Holy Spirit. We are not watching to understand the timing of events; we are watching to keep our eyes on the Holy Spirit so that we can move when He gives us the order. He will be the one to give us the first signal that the Master is returning. In the meantime, we are to do the work our Lord left for us. Being an assistant doorkeeper does not qualify as a legitimate work.

Verse 35 reveals that watching does not entail researching the time of day the Lord will come. It will not necessarily be when it's darkest or when it's lightest. If you already have theories on that, make sure you have heard from the Doorkeeper and not just from eschatalogical researchers.

Once we understand that the Holy Spirit is the Doorkeeper (this is another of His important roles), verse 36 comes alive to us. When the Lord does return, it will be *"suddenly,"* and, therefore, there is a danger of being found *"sleeping."* If this were not true, He would not have warned us of it.

The Lord's final emphatic command, *"Watch!"* alerts us to the need to maintain a constant relationship with the Holy Spirit. If we stay in relationship with Him, He will keep us alert and awake. It has been promised that *"He will show you things to come"* (John 16:13). If we wrongfully interpret the Lord's command to watch as meaning that we must continually be checking outside to see what time of day it is, we will not be able to properly do the work He has left us. The Doorkeeper is our key to the Master's return. If we stay in an active actual relationship with Him, we have nothing to fear. We will not be surprised by end-time events.

The other passage of Scripture that leads many to believe that they must "figure it all out" is found in 1 Thessalonians 5. In this chapter, Paul described *"the Day of the Lord."* In verse 4, he said, *"But you, brethren, are not in darkness, so that this day should overtake you as a thief."* In verse 2, however, Paul had already stated that the Day of the Lord would come *"as a thief in the night."* Is this a contradiction? No.

The great unknown is not that the Lord is coming back, but WHEN He is coming. His desire is to protect us from the surprise of this unknown. We must remember that the Holy Spirit is the Doorkeeper, who is our buffer for all surprises. It's not research, not study, not knowing the Hebrew calendar, not understanding who the "ten horns" are, not knowing who the antichrist is, not knowing how many years it's been since Israel became a nation, and not knowing about a thousand other things that I could mention.

The Holy Spirit is our teacher, and He doesn't use our intelligence to teach us (as many seem to think). He teaches our spirits, which then need to teach our minds *"the wisdom that is from above."* In order to be a watcher, we do not need to figure out a single mystery from the book of Revelation. The Holy Spirit can reveal each event to us as the need arises. He will say to us, "This is that which was spoken in the book of Revelation … ."

Totally apart from the prophetic speculations of our day, there are prophetic scriptures that the Holy Spirit Himself is highlighting to us. He is releasing significant prophetic information to the Body, and these insights are to be embraced. The remarkable thing about some passages that I want to make mention of is that they cannot be linked to one man or one movement as their source. As I travel to many other countries, I find it noteworthy that the Holy Spirit is spotlighting the same prophetic passages to His people every-where. These revelations are imparting an incredible fresh anointing to the Church.

The most powerful of these passages is from Isaiah:

> *Arise, shine;*
> *For your light has come!*
> *And the glory of the Lord is risen upon you.*
> *For behold, the darkness shall cover the earth,*
> *And deep darkness the people;*
> *But the Lord will arise over you,*
> *And His glory will be seen upon you.*   Isaiah 60:1-2

These first two words are imperatives that the Holy Spirit is releas-ing into our spirits. This word *"arise"* is from the Hebrew word *quwm*, which, among other things, means "to rise … and accomplish, and be clear, and confirm, and strengthen, and succeed." This word *"shine"* is from the Hebrew word *owr*, which means "to be luminous, to be glorious, to set on fire and to show light." This is the specified time for this to happen. What is the proof for this? It is certainly not a spiritual mathematical formula or something that prophecy research has revealed. It is simply what the Holy Spirit is speaking to in-tune believers everywhere. We can choose not to believe it, and, in that case, nothing will be released into our spirits. If we choose to believe it, then the *"shine"* will begin to manifest in our lives.

Verse 2 gives us a timetable of just when this imperative was to be upon us. It was when *"darkness"* and *"deep darkness"* were present. This is when the Lord will arise over us and when His glory will be seen upon us. The worse things become in the world around us, the more we are to position ourselves to shine.

The rest of this chapter 60 is also being highlighted by the Lord to His people these days. It describes the various ways we will *"arise and shine."* *"Being caught up in the sky"* (1 Thessalonians 4:17) surely cannot happen until this prophetic period has been realized. That is why the Holy Spirit is now highlighting this everywhere. He is preparing us for the next great event.

While we have been concentrating on departing from this world, the Lord has been trying to prepare us to shine in this world. Those who fail to grasp this truth may be terrified to see just how much darkness the Lord allows us to coexist with. If we expect the darkness, we cannot be terrified by it, and we should not be terrified by it. The Lord lets us know that there will be even more glory seen upon us in the darkness. Where there is more sin, He releases more of His grace. Darkness cannot overtake light, and therein lies our faith, hope and confidence.

God is already showing forth His glory in some very unusual ways. Recently, I attended a meeting with the Baptist evangelist Bob Shattles. God has been using him and displaying many signs and wonders in his ministry. The most notable of these signs has been the gold dust phenomenon that many are reporting today. As Bob was preaching, sparkling bits of golden substance popped out on his face and his coat, and their intensity increased as he ministered.

After the meeting that night, I curiously followed the trail of where Bob Shattles had walked and where he sat. Golden sparkles were everywhere in the vicinity. They were on the chairs, on the pulpit, and on the carpet. While he was still praying for everyone, I noticed his Bible lying on the platform. I decided to go check it out for more gold. Sure enough, there were gold specks on his Bible and inside of it.

I was curious as to what Isaiah 60 might look like in Bob's Bible, so I opened it thinking that I would turn there. Amazingly, the Bible opened to Isaiah 60, and that page was covered with golden specks. The margin of the page had at least a quarter of an inch of gold dust around it. I looked at other places in his Bible, but I found no other pages that were so intensely marked with the gold dust.

I am sure that many will doubt what I am saying, but I can provide the names of at least ten witnesses to these facts. We threw the gold dust into the air and were covered by it as it rained down upon us. It took some of us days to get all the gold dust out of our hair and skin. This sign and wonder only confirmed to me that the Holy Spirit is highlighting this passage for His people today.

Through this phenomenon, the Lord is reminding us that He is Jehovah-Jireh, God our Provider. One of the marks of the Lord's glory upon us in these days will be supernatural provision. Isaiah continued:

> *Then you shall see and become radiant,*
> *And your heart shall swell with joy;*
> *Because the abundance of the sea shall be turned to you,*
> *THE WEALTH OF THE GENTILES [HEATHEN] SHALL COME TO YOU.*
> *They shall bring GOLD and incense.*
> *To bring your sons from afar,*
> *THEIR SILVER AND GOLD with them.*
> *That men may bring to you THE WEALTH OF THE GENTILES [HEATHEN].*
> *Instead of bronze I will bring GOLD.*
>
> Isaiah 60:5-6 and 9, 11 and 17

I believe that the reason the gold dust appears on the pages of Isaiah 60 is that God is giving us a down payment on this prophetic promise.

Isaiah 61 is another portion that is being emphasized by the Holy Spirit. The first three verses are being strongly highlighted these days:

> *The Spirit of the Lord God is upon Me,*
> *Because the Lord has anointed Me*
> *To preach good tidings to the poor;*
> *He has sent Me to heal the brokenhearted,*
> *To proclaim liberty to the captives,*
> *And the opening of the prison to those who are bound;*
> *To proclaim the acceptable year of the Lord,*
> *And the day of vengeance of our God;*
> *To comfort all who mourn,*
> *To console those who mourn in Zion,*
> *To give them beauty for ashes,*
> *The oil of joy for mourning,*
> *The garment of praise for the spirit of heaviness;*
> *That they may be called trees of righteousness,*
> *The planting of the Lord, that He may be glorified.* Isaiah 61:1-3

This passage further explains our command to *"arise and shine."* Verse 2 shows us the simultaneous working of God's favor and His judgment — vengeance on the Lord's enemies and *"the acceptable year"* (meaning favor) for God's people.

The promise of prosperity continues:

> *You shall eat of the riches of the Gentiles [heathen], and in their glory you shall boast.*
> *Therefore in their land they shall possess double.*
> *All who see them shall acknowledge them, that they are the posterity whom the Lord has blessed.* Verses 6-7 and 9

Provision will no longer be a problem for true ministers of God. This will be an aspect of the glory that will be *"seen upon [us]."*

Chapter four of Malachi is another portion of scripture that is being highlighted by the Holy Spirit in these days:

> *"For behold, the day is coming,*
> *Burning like an oven,*
> *And all the proud, yes all who do wickedly will be stubble.*
> *And the day which is coming shall burn them up,"*
> *Says the Lord of hosts,*
> *"That will leave them neither root nor branch.*
> *But to you who fear My name*
> *The Sun of Righteousness shall arise*
> *With healing in His wings;*
> *And you shall go out*
> *And grow fat like stall-fed calves.*
> *You shall trample the wicked,*
> *For they shall be ashes under the soles of your feet*
> *On the day that I do this,"*
> *Says the Lord of hosts.* Malachi 4:1-3

Notice several key elements in this promise. The *"day"* that is coming will be *"burning like an oven."* It will be terrible for the proud and those who are living wickedly. Apparently, *"those who fear [God's] name"* will still be around, and it will be a great time for them. They will grow *"fat like stall-fed calves."* Obviously, none of this has yet happened, so we understand that it is for the near future. This is the reason the Holy Spirit is now highlighting it.

Haggai 2:6-9 is another powerful prophetic scripture that the Holy Spirit is speaking to many all over the world:

> *For thus says the Lord of hosts: "Once more (it is a little while) I will shake heaven and earth, the sea and dry land; and I will shake all nations, and they shall come to the Desire of All Nations, and I will fill this temple with glory," says the Lord of hosts.*

"The silver is Mine, AND THE GOLD IS MINE [emphasis mine]," says the Lord of hosts.
"The glory of this latter temple shall be greater than the former," says the Lord of hosts. "And in this place I will give peace," says the Lord of hosts.

Haggai 2:6-9

There are several things to highlight in this passage. A great shaking is coming. Yet, rather than removing His people, the Lord will fill His temple with unmatched glory. In the former glory, there were times when even the priests could not function because of the manifestation of the glory (see 1 Kings 8:10-11). We have a long way to go to even match this former glory, but an even greater glory is coming. This coming glory will be an actual physical presence, but it will also produce all the good effects promised by Isaiah 60 and 61.

Notice (in verse 8) what is stuck right in the middle of these glory verses. It is a statement reminding us: *"THE GOLD IS MINE."* Once again, it is no coincidence that glory and gold are found in the same prophecy. The gold we are now seeing is a sign that the glory is not far behind.

To review every prophetic passage that the Spirit is highlighting today would require another book. Let me suggest several passages that the reader may wish to search out: Joel 2:23-32, Psalm 37, Zechariah 9:9-17, Ezekiel 37, Acts 2:17-21 and Romans 8:18-26.

I realize that many of these passages have an application for natural Israel, and Israel will indeed be part of God's wonderful plan of restoration. The children of Israel are modern-day prodigal sons, and the Father's heart has always longed for their return to Him. His love will ultimately win them back.

The people of Israel do not have an exemption that will allow them to experience restoration without repentance. Their regrafting into the Vine will be complete when they have finally turned to Jesus. I don't claim to have some great insight into this process and how it will unfold, but I know that we must be careful not to have the attitude of the elder brother. God has a plan for the ultimate restoration of at least a significant remnant of Israel, and when it happens, Heaven will rejoice. Woe to those who have created a theology that precludes the prodigal son from coming back home!

Now, I must return to the question I posed at the outset of the chapter: "What is holding YOU back?" I trust that the message of this book has served to rid you of many of the weights that have held you back and kept you from running the race. Satan will use anything he can to keep you from being an effective Christian. His tools are many: sin, the flesh, demons, sickness, devouring your provision, etc. He also uses "good" things, religious things. He tries to overload you and overwork you so that you will be too burdened to be effective. He truly is *a roaring lion who walks about seeking whom he may devour*(1 Peter 5:8).

In the well-known Parable of the Talents (see Matthew 25), burying our talents was shown to be an absolutely unacceptable action. This is still one of Satan's most powerful tools. He causes us to compare ourselves with those who have twice or five times the talents we have, and he convinces us to bury what little we have. He never tells us that those who have more talents got them by risking the little they originally had.

Many of us have fallen for Satan's trick. We are fasting, praying and interceding for more talents so that we can begin to do something for God. In the meantime, we have buried the one talent God has given us, and we feel that we can do nothing until we have more. We go to conference after conference looking for a special prophetic word or supernatural experience that will bring us to the two-talent level or, even better, the five-talent level. We are sure that we just don't have enough to get started yet. What a lie! And too many of us have swallowed it.

We feel that we must have famous people lay hands on us, acknowledge us, or in some other way validate us. We are so insecure that we need such recognition before we will use the deposit that the Lord has made in us. That's why it is often difficult to get Christians to shine in public places. Since their pastor won't see what they do there, they feel that they might as well save their energy for where someone will notice.

True promotion is of the Lord, yet we continue to do our good works before men, hoping to receive their recognition. Although men can promote us in our present church system, the only promotion that lasts is from the Lord. All other promotion is fleeting and will one day be tried by fire.

Often the leaders of the churches we attend do, in fact, overlook our true talents. Your church and your pastor may have no idea that you are loaded with heavenly talents. Although that fact may inhibit the display of your talents in the church setting, it need not inhibit their display in the marketplace. If you are truly prophetic, there is no better place to exercise your gifts than outside of the church.

Let the Lord validate you. If no one recognizes the gift of healing in you, that should not stop you from finding sick people to pray for. Go to the hospitals and nursing homes. Put an ad in the newspaper stating that you pray for the sick. Do whatever it takes. Avoid causing discord with your spiritual leaders and fellow believers, and work within the church system when you can, but whatever you do, don't bury your talents.

There is a world of sick and dying people who desperately need the light that shines through us. Every one of us needs to be risking our talents for the sake of the Kingdom. Many are willing to risk their talents for recognition or promotion, but that does not fulfill our responsibility of stewardship. Use what the Lord has given you, and use it everywhere you can.

It may be that the only gift you presently see in yourself is the boldness to tell someone that God loves them. If you will totally risk and invest that talent, more will be given to you. Meanwhile, that little talent may be powerfully used by God to precipitate life-changing encounters in people's lives.

Satan may grudgingly recognize our talents, but he will then try to convince us that, at the very least, we should bury them UNTIL all the sin is out of our lives. He tries to deceive us into working up our "righteousness resume," and it's never good enough. When we can feel good about ourselves, he tells us, THEN we will use our talents. However, the Proverbs teach us:

> *For a righteous man may fall seven times and rise again.*
>
> Proverbs 24:16

That single verse destroys the theology of many. "If a man is truly *'righteous,'* " they reason, *"how can he 'fall seven times'?"* Righteousness is not a behavior performance. Righteousness means being clothed with the justness of the Lord Jesus Christ. Righteousness is not a product of our own goodness. Some of those who risk their talents the most take some very obvious falls. To the degree that they *"rise again"* in Christ's work of atonement, to that degree they are *"righteous."* Getting back up when we have fallen is one of the greatest signs of true righteousness.

We all know dozens of people who have fallen and can't seem to get back up. Sometimes it is because of their belief that they need to be personally righteous. If they can only get their personal righteousness back in order, they believe, they can get back up. If you are one of those who has been waylaid by this deception, just get back up in the name of Jesus. He is your righteousness. You need no other clothing.

Those who are in public ministry and fall have a more serious problem. They lose their credibility. It may take them longer to get back into the saddle. It is not necessary to immediately step back into the spotlight. There are other ways to get up. Whether you are a minister or a layperson, never wallow in your failure. Don't allow that which God has placed in you to remain buried because of your own weakness. The only thing that can permanently disqualify you from being used of God is your refusal to *"rise again."* (Of course, the door to rising again is true repentance.) Although it is possible to disqualify yourself in just how you are used, there are always other outlets for your talents. Never be guilty of burying them.

The prophet Amos warned:

"Behold, the days are coming,"
says the Lord,
"When the plowman shall overtake the reaper."   Amos 9:13

This verse lies in the middle of many other promises of restoration. It is a prophetic description of the end-time harvest. *The Living Bible* renders it this way:

The time will come when there will be such abundance of crops, that the harvest time will scarcely end before the farmer starts again to sow another crop.

Agriculturally speaking, fall is usually harvest time. Fall is followed by winter, a downtime when the ground generally rests. In the spring, the farmer plows his field that has sat idle all winter, and he then sows it again. What Amos is saying is that there is coming a harvest with no downtime. The *"plowman"* will have to work around the year. No sooner will a harvest take place than preparations for another will have to be made. Harvesters will have a hard time keeping up with the coming waves of grain.

This time is nearly upon us, and we will soon need all available workers in the field. The end-time harvest of souls will require that every true Christian participate. Don't be caught trying to build up your personal righteousness resume while thousands of souls risk rotting for lack of attention (that's what happens to crops when there are not enough harvesters).

You may indeed be fallen, but you need to get up quickly and help with the harvest. Repent quickly and rise again so that you can be about your Father's business. The joy of the harvest awaits you (see Isaiah 9:3). Lay aside every weight and run the race set before you, looking to Jesus the Author and Finisher of our faith. Don't allow sin and condemnation to make you a vessel of dishonor, but rather rise again through the price Jesus Christ paid with His own blood. And when you do, be prepared to do *"every good work"* (Titus 2:21).

Learn to clothe yourself in the righteousness of Jesus Christ, and learn to operate boldly in His righteousness, not your own. Boldly come to the throne of grace, not because you have fasted forty days or because you have prayed three hours a day or because you have given away everything you possessed or because of anything else that originates in you. Your access to God's throne is based on the profound understanding and appropriating of His complete sacrifice for you on Calvary.

Go ahead, what's holding YOU back? Set it aside and go for all that God has for you.

CHAPTER 12

THESE SIGNS WILL FOLLOW
THOSE WHO BELIEVE

An evil and adulterous generation seeks after a sign.   Matthew 12:39

Before bringing this book to a conclusion, I feel that I need to address an area of great friction currently in the Body of Christ. Many Christians have a deep-seated fear of being deceived with false signs and wonders, and this often causes them to reject the true signs God gives. Some have even accused me of being a performer of lying signs and wonders.

Jesus did warn men of being deceived in this way. He even said that *"an evil and adulterous generation seeks after a sign."* But now this phrase is being used by Christians who doubt that God still does miracles today. The verse has been twisted and turned to say a lot of things that it does not say. The implication has been that it is evil to even seek a sign, and nothing could be further from the truth.

This same Jesus said:

> *And these signs will follow those WHO BELIEVE [emphasis mine]: In My name they will cast out demons; they will speak with new tongues: they will take up serpents; and if they drink anything deadly, it will by no means hurt them; they will lay hands on the sick, and they will recover.*
> Mark 16:17-18

So was Jesus against signs? In no way. It is necessary to look more closely at the passages where Jesus criticized the Pharisees and the signs they sought. In the contemporary religious culture of Jesus' day, it was a relatively common occurrence for new so-called "messiahs" to spring up from time to time. These men served to muddy the waters for Jesus' appearing. Each of them was assigned credibility based on the signs he performed. Whoever had the best magic would usually gather the greatest following. Most of the messiahs would eventually be proven frauds, as their tricks would be uncovered (they were little more than magicians). Some of the messiahs possessed enough power to draw crowds of hundreds, but none had been impressive enough to garner unanimous support.

All this created a bizarre culture of attention to the performing of signs. Any new rumored or prospective messiah was expected to first show a sign to legitimize his claim. Those who witnessed the sign would then determine if they had seen better or not. It was in this climate that the religious leaders of the day approached Jesus:

> *Then the Pharisees and Sadducees came, and testing Him asked that He would show them a sign from heaven.*   Matthew 16:1

> *Then some of the scribes and Pharisees answered, saying, "Teacher, we want to see a sign from You."*   Matthew 12:38

Understanding this context causes us to also understand the severe wording of Jesus' response. He was refusing to play the Pharisees' game. He could have produced any number of unmatchable signs. For instance, Jesus could have called ten thousand angels and "slam-dunked the competition." If He had done that, no one would have been able to doubt His Messiahship. Jesus, however, chose not to come in overwhelming power; He came in confirming power. He preached *"with signs following,"* not preceding. He released enough power that it attested to the fact that He was from above and sent by God (see Acts 2:22); then He left it to men to believe or not believe.

Jesus never tried to overwhelm men with His power. For instance, He could have pulled the nails out of His hands and removed Himself from the cross. Then He could have shot bolts of lightning at those who were crucifying Him. He could have overwhelmed the world into submission by a sheer display of brute force. Why didn't He do that? Our heavenly Father desires to provide access to Heaven to those who respond with faith.

God's Word declares: *"Without FAITH it is impossible to please Him"* (Hebrews 11:6). The ability to reach out in FAITH reveals a heart saturated by the urgings of the Holy Spirit. If God revealed Himself in even a fraction of His glory and power, all creation would immediately bow. Hearts that responded in this way, however, would not have been won over by love. What the Father cannot win over by love, He cannot trust. And what the Father cannot trust cannot abide with Him. He will not risk having another Lucifer. He wants those who choose Him to do so because they love Him.

Jesus did many signs, but He did them so that men might believe, not just to satisfy the curious:

> *And truly Jesus did many other signs in the presence of His disciples, which are not written in this book; but these are written that you may believe that Jesus is the Christ, the Son of God, and that believing you may have life in His name.* John 20:30-31

Jesus clearly wasn't against signs. He performed many of them Himself.

The verses previous to this declaration tell of Jesus' encounter with Thomas after He was risen. Because Thomas doubted, Jesus allowed him to touch the hollow of His hand to prove that He was Jesus. Signs, then, are a weapon against unbelief. They are never present to substitute the need for faith. They are a weapon against that which smothers faith. Once Thomas' unbelief had been disabled, his faith was able to take hold once again.

Many of those who now accept signs and wonders as part of God's plan for today at one time did not. Unbelief gripped them, as it had Thomas. Once they experienced God's power for themselves, however, all doubt was removed.

Some Christians are mocking what they call "experiential Christianity," not understanding that it often takes an experience to fully disable unbelief. We could have a lengthy debate on whether a glass of water holds hot water or cold water. We could theorize and theologize and get many scriptures to back up both arguments. However, at some point, actual proof of truth would be in sticking a finger into the water. This "experience" would reveal which theology was correct and which was not. Experience is not a substitute theology; rather, it is that which proves the correct theology. Experience can quickly change our theology, and if that happens, it means that we have been believing a lie.

Because I have experienced miraculous healing, I know that healing is for today. It wouldn't matter how many dispensational charts someone lined up to show me that it wasn't, I would not be convinced. I have already touched it, so I know it's real. Once you have watched a blind man receive his sight, it would be hard to convince you that God no longer heals. My experience protects me from the erroneous idea that miracles ceased when the apostles died. My experience confirms my theology.

It is very sad when Christians allow themselves to be caught up in criticism of God's signs and wonders. It is bad enough when the world rejects Him, but when Christians do it, it surely must break His heart. Rather than open their hearts to His wonders, they call what they are seeing *"lying signs and wonders."* If you are one of those who have been bound by this kind of unbelief, you can be set free. Right now, allow the Holy Spirit to have a new place in your heart.

My purpose in stating all this is not just to win an argument. The fact is that there is too much to be done for us to be arguing over the way God works. But we need all the weaponry that God has provided to defeat our common enemy. God is not the great "I WAS"; He is the great "I AM."

These Signs Will Follow Those Who Believe

Jesus brought a serious indictment against believers who aid the enemy through their unbelief:

> *Woe to you, Chorazin! Woe to you Bethsaida! For if the mighty works which were done in you had been done in Tyre and Sidon, they would have repented a great while ago, sitting in sackcloth and ashes. But it will be more tolerable for Tyre and Sidon at the judgment than for you. And you, Capernaum, who are exalted to heaven, will be thrust down to Hades. He who hears you hears Me, he who rejects you rejects Me, and he who rejects Me rejects Him who sent Me.*   Luke 10:13-16

Once we have been exposed to God's *"mighty works,"* we have an increased responsibility.

We must get used to signs and wonders now, for there will soon be an exponential increase in their release upon the Earth. The purpose of this new wave of God's mighty works is to raise accountability across the board. Hear the warning: *"He who hears you hears Me, he who rejects Me rejects Him who sent Me."* If you choose to reject the coming outpouring of the Holy Spirit, you not only will be rejecting the Holy Spirit or the vessel He uses, but you will also be rejecting Him who sends the outpouring. How will you face Him in eternity? And what will you say?

THE COUNTERFEIT PRINCIPLE

> *For false christs and false prophets will arise and show great signs and wonders, so as to deceive, if possible, even the elect.*   Matthew 24:24

There *is* a need to be cautious. Here, Jesus was speaking of the end-times, and He showed that *"signs and wonders"* will also be used to deceive many in the days to come. There *is* such a thing as counterfeit signs and wonders, and if such *"signs and wonders"* could present a challenge even to *"the elect,"* that is a sobering thought. The solution, however, cannot be to avoid all manifestations of power, as some would suggest. Instead, I have come up with a

Counterfeit Principle that I believe will help many to know the true from the false. *Just because the counterfeit looks very similar to the real is no reason to get rid of the real.*

Consider the hundred-dollar bill. It is one of the most counter-feited bills in the world. When I want to use one, in many countries I am forced to go through a terrible ordeal. These bills are immedi-ately looked upon with suspicion, and before banks or money changers are willing to hand over the equivalent exchange rate in their local currency, they first want to make a very thorough examination of my bill. I have been tempted never to carry hun-dred-dollar bills, but sometimes the hundred-dollar bill is just the right size for the job. I like hundred-dollar bills. There are many more good ones than bad ones, and I never throw them away.

The same is true in the spiritual. When I was in Peru on one of my trips, a man was conducting what looked like a renewal meeting. He would lay hands on individuals, and they would fall over — much like we see happening in many places as people are touched by the Holy Spirit. Some of those he prayed for went into ecstatic trances, and it seemed very similar to what we have seen happen in the Spirit. The difference, though, was that this man was not even a Christian. He did not exalt the name of Jesus, and he didn't invite the Holy Spirit to minister. He was a New Age shaman who spoke of many impersonal "powers." He was actually operating in de-monic power. This was indeed a challenging counterfeit, but the fact that it exists has not tempted me to stop asking the Holy Spirit to minister to people in my meetings. I refuse to toss aside the good, simply because bad exists.

I once wondered what would be involved in detecting counterfeit money. *Would I have to study all the counterfeit bills?* What I learned is that just the opposite is true. Those who train to detect counterfeit money spend their time examining the real thing. Once they know the real money well enough, it becomes easy for them to detect a counterfeit.

We have somehow developed an entire field of workers in Chris-tianity who go about this thing all backward. They spend all their time studying fakes and counterfeits, and when they see the real, it just looks like another counterfeit to them. These people firmly believe that they are doing a service to the Body of Christ, but some of the conclusions they reach are totally absurd.

For instance, they come to the conclusion that Christians should never "meditate" because certain Eastern religions practice what they call "meditation." But David spoke often of meditating in his psalms, and God inspired those words. Who are we helping if we eliminate the real to avoid having a counterfeit?

We should not speak in tongues, they now tell us, because some Hindus and African tribes do it in their occultic ceremonies. So, their conclusion is that we have to declare, "Out with the real!" just because someone has a fake. That doesn't make sense.

People like these now declare that it is wrong for us to passionately dance before God because the world dances and because it has been discovered that certain demonic worshipers do, too. So, they want us to say, "Out with the real!" I, for one, choose to dance before the Lord with all my might — just as David did. I know that it pleases the heart of God when we dance to His glory.

One by one, we are discovering that every supernatural manifestation of the Holy Spirit has a counterfeit. Should this be a surprise to us? The effect of those who would try to protect us from all the evils is to rob us of God's power in our lives. If we allow this to happen, we will become stripped of everything meaningful and be left in spiritual nakedness.

Don't be robbed in this area. Expect every good thing from Heaven to be counterfeited by the enemy, but keep on enjoying the true blessings that God has given to you.

Lying signs and wonders have been around for thousands of years. When Moses had his brother Aaron cast down his rod before Pharaoh, and it became a serpent (so that Pharaoh would see God's power), the sorcerers and magicians of Egypt were able to reproduce that same sign. Moses turned the rivers of Egypt to blood, and the magicians did the same thing. Moses and Aaron produced the plague of frogs, and the magicians did the same through their enchantments. Just because a sign can be counterfeited doesn't mean that it's not a true sign. Though a false sign *does* muddy the waters, that is no reason for us to back off from certain signs and manifestations just because they can be demonically duplicated.

Satan does not have creative powers; he only has counterfeiting powers. He will always see what God is doing and use that as the master copy from which to produce his counterfeit. He floods the market with fakes, hoping that you will become discouraged and avoid the real.

If studying counterfeits is not what we need to do, then what will work? The answer is true discernment. We can only know the true and the false by the Spirit. There is no other way. Discernment is like the sense of smell. At times, what your eyes see has to be overlooked because of what your sense of smell is telling you. There is a point at which refrigerated meats go bad. Meat may look exactly the same as it did when it was fresh, but you can't trust your sight in such matters. It's too dangerous. It's the smell that tells you that the meat must definitely be thrown out.

There is also the case of cooked food that looks disgusting but tastes wonderful. If you went by what you see, you might not even want to taste it. If you smell it, however, you will realize that it is very good.

The first time I saw refried beans, they were visually distasteful to me. The smell I picked up, however, told me that what I was about to eat was going to be good. Later, after I ate refried beans for the first time, I no longer had to override my sense of sight. I now knew that the beans were good, and they actually began to look good to me.

One of the problems with many of those who have set themselves up as experts on the supernatural is that they have little or no spiritual discernment. They decide that something is good or bad based solely on what they see. Because they have no spiritual smelling, they cannot judge any other way. If they see two meetings with supernatural manifestations that look much the same, they will judge them both good or both bad, based on what their eyes tell them. One of these meetings could be exalting Satan, and one of them could be exalting Jesus. To those who lack discernment, however, they would be identical.

I once attended that mega-church I mentioned, and it was almost perfect visually. It was one of the fastest-growing churches in America. There was a special ministry that worked with the inner city youth, one that worked with homosexuals, drug addicts and prostitutes, and another that worked with abused women. The pastor would often have tears in his eyes as he made the altar call and invited sinners to come to Jesus. He would sometimes hold hurting people in his arms and weep with them. He had a great relationship with children, and they loved to be near him. I thought I was in the greatest church in the world with the greatest man of God as my pastor.

As it turned out, the church was not what it appeared to be. The pastor was found to be having adulterous relationships with several women of the church at the same time. A female pastor, female members of the worship team and other staff persons were involved in this sin. Abortion, drug use and wife-swapping were just a few of the evils found within the inner circle of the church.

I was stunned when it all came to light. I had been moving up in the leadership of the church myself and had become very familiar with many of the individuals in the ring of incredibly depraved sin. Many of them were my close neighbors and friends.

The thing that shocked me most was the fact that I had been part of that church for five years and still had not discerned the problems. It was because I was still using the mental, visual method of discernment and not the more sensitive smelling in the Spirit.

After my wife and I left the church, we met people who had one time considered going to this church but just couldn't. To them, "something stank." A spiritual stink is not something you can easily explain theologically, just as you cannot explain why your nose knows when food has gone bad:

"Isn't that a great cut of meat?"

"Yes."

"Isn't it cut in the perfect size?"

"Yes, it is."

"Isn't the date on it okay?"

"It is, but for some reason, it stinks."

When we come to that conclusion, not many of us would still want to eat it. We have learned to trust our sense of smell above our visual sense — when it comes to ingesting food.

True spiritual discernment is not based on fear. A fear of being deceived is not a proper basis for discernment. Nor is any other kind of fear. There is an entire pseudo-discernment movement composed of those influenced by a culture of paranoia, suspicion, slander and gossip. If you are a mistrustful person, you have almost no chance of being plugged into true discernment. You might accidentally trip onto uncovering something, but it would be an accident. If you are suspicious and mistrustful about everything and everybody, you will happen upon enough human frailty to keep yourself deceived into believing that you are a discerner. True discernment, however, comes out of a living, confident relationship with the Holy Spirit.

The Spirit is our Teacher. He and He alone is our hookup to spiritual smell. The more we rely on Him teaching us, the more discernment we can access. The more we rely on our thought processes, the more we cease to discern and the more open we become to deception.

Sometimes our mind alone might be able to recognize spiritual rot. In cases such as the Branch Davidians and the Jim Jones group in Guyana, it didn't take much discernment to recognize that they were false cults. It's like being able to see worms in spoiled meat. At that point, you don't even need to exercise your sense of smell. Even your visual sense tells you that the meat is rotten. But anyone in the Body of Christ who leans only on his or her mind is likely to be thoroughly deceived when the end-time lying signs and wonders really begin to appear. Your only protection in that time will be true humility and a total reliance upon the Holy Spirit.

You might eat poisoned food if your spiritual nose (the Holy Spirit) is not in His place of pre-eminence. It doesn't matter what

New Agers do or don't do. It doesn't matter what shamans do or don't do. It doesn't matter what voodoo practitioners do or don't do. It doesn't matter what Buddhists do or don't do. It doesn't matter what Hindus do or don't do. It doesn't matter what tribal rituals are taking place in Africa. It doesn't matter what Mormons, Jehovah's Witnesses, Masons or even satanists are doing. We don't need to research any of these groups to make sure we don't stray into their territory.

Demonic worship in all its various forms will always counterfeit the true. It would prove nothing if any of these groups began to have the same manifestations that we experience. Ours are manifestations of the Holy Spirit, and theirs are counterfeits, inspired by evil spirits. They might be able to duplicate some signs and not others (as with Moses and the magicians of Egypt). If, however, we exalt the name of Jesus and invite the Holy Spirit into our meetings, we can have confidence that the power that is demonstrated (with its accompanying manifestations) is from God.

Again, Jesus clearly taught:

> *If a son asks for bread from any father among you, will he give him a stone? Or if he asks for a fish, will he give him a serpent instead of a fish? Or if he asks for an egg, will he offer him a scorpion? If you then, being evil, know how to give good gifts to your children, HOW MUCH MORE WILL YOUR HEAVENLY FATHER GIVE THE HOLY SPIRIT TO THOSE WHO ASK HIM!*   Luke 11:11-13

This promise comforts us with the assurance that if we invite the Holy Spirit into our midst, what comes will, in fact, be the Holy Spirit.

The promise was given specifically about the Holy Spirit. Jesus was not saying that if we ask God for a BMW, then He would not give us a Ford Pinto. He was specifically talking about the Holy Spirit. If we ask for Him, we will not receive a serpent or a scorpion, both of which are demonic symbols. If we invite the Holy Spirit into our midst, the Father promises that He will not allow anything evil to come to us.

It is true that when the Holy Spirit comes, He may reveal the presence of existing serpents and scorpions that need to be chased out. That is something very different. Also, some immature believers may at times fake some manifestations, but we can know that the Holy Spirit is presiding and rest in that knowledge.

If we did not have this assurance, we would be afraid to ever yield ourselves to the Holy Spirit. We would always want to remain in charge. But it is impossible to be filled with that which we do not yield to. So, if we want to be filled with the Holy Spirit, we must yield to Him. This requires a laying down of one's defenses. It necessitates that we become vulnerable in a state of surrender.

This word "yield" means "to surrender or relinquish to the physical control of another." Many Christians have not yet yielded to the Holy Spirit. How, then, can they hope to be filled with Him. Yielding to the Holy Spirit means surrendering control of the mechanisms of our minds to Him. It is impossible to be scanning for error and yielding simultaneously. At some point, we must begin to trust the Father enough to fulfill His promise of Luke 11. If we believe that God is big enough to keep His word, we should have nothing to fear in this regard.

WHAT CAN WE CONCLUDE?

Since the purpose of this book is to free men and women from their limited thinking and let them know that they are qualified to be used by God, I felt it was necessary to broach this subject of lying signs and wonders. As many of you step out into the new boldness that is ignited in you by the truths of this book, you will encounter people who will attempt to rob you of the manifestations of the Holy Spirit in your life. They will do it by casting aspersions on what is happening to you and insinuating that it just might be demonic or occultic. If you don't know how to defend yourself in those moments, you could be seduced to giving up the great things God is placing into your spirit.

Don't let that happen! God will use a wide range of supernatural manifestations in the days ahead, and we must not lose the privilege of utilizing His power just because some occultic group has been demonically inspired to counterfeit His works. Paul wrote very strongly to the Galatian believers:

> *But this occurred because of false brethren secretly brought in (who came in by stealth to spy out our liberty which we have in Christ Jesus, that they might bring us into bondage), to whom we did not yield submission even for an hour, that the truth of the gospel might continue with you.*
>   Galatians 2:4-5

The situation was a little different in Galatia, but the admonition is sound for the case of which we speak. If we let them do it, *"false brethren"* will *"spy out our liberty"* and attempt to *"bring us into bondage."* We must not let that happen. There is a liberty that the Holy Spirit brings to His church that Satan hates and would like to hinder in any way he can. Even in churches that allow some manifestation of the Holy Spirit, he would like to force us to place "restrictions" on what God can do.

In some churches now, the Holy Spirit is free to manifest a spirit of repentance, but not one of joy. Supernatural weeping is accepted, but supernatural laughing is not. In other churches, it's just the reverse. This ought not to be. We should want all that God has for us. Paul warned:

> *Stand fast therefore in the liberty by which Christ has made us free, and do not be entangled again with a yoke of bondage.*   Galatians 5:1

God is bringing new freedom to His Body. Please make sure you are not being more "sober and orderly" than He is.

The hour in which we live is a very serious one, and things will soon become much more serious for us, but that does not mean that we must lose our joy and our exuberance in the Holy Spirit. When Paul was in jail in Philippi, he wasn't sad or "serious" or "sober." He was rejoicing, and it was that rejoicing that caused the foundations of the prison to shake and ultimately to set the prisoners free. After all, what is the Kingdom of God? Paul wrote:

> *For the kingdom of God is not food and drink, but righteousness and peace and JOY IN THE HOLY SPIRIT.*   Romans 14:17

I encourage you to receive all the benefits of the joy the Holy Spirit offers. We will all need the strength this joy affords us in the days to come. David declared:

> *In Your presence is fullness of joy; and at Your right hand are pleasures for evermore.*   Psalm 16:11

As the latter-day outpouring of the Holy Spirit increases, expect the joy to increase. Yes, the days will be difficult, but we are not of this world. Enjoy the new wine God is offering. Enjoy the gold dust He is raining down on His people. Enjoy seeing oil miraculously form in your hands. Rejoice in the supernatural fillings God is placing in your teeth. Insist on enjoying every manifestation of His power. Insist on allowing every sign and wonder that God wants to give you.

This is the season in which our Father has chosen to release favor on His children and judgment on those who refuse to bow before Him. Don't refuse any mark of His favor. These will become your most powerful tools for evangelism, for bringing in the harvest of the last days.

May an army of happy, humble donkeys arise all across the land, and may the King of Kings and Lord of Lords use them to make His Triumphal Entry.

Amen!

For you see your calling, brethren, that not many wise according to the flesh, not many mighty, not many noble, are called. But God has chosen the foolish things of the world to put to shame the wise, and God has chosen the weak things of the world to put to shame the things which are mighty; and the base things of the world and the things which are despised God has chosen, and the things which are not, to bring to nothing the things that are, that no flesh should glory in His presence.

1 Corinthians 1:26-29

Ministry Address:

**John Enlow
Refuge to the Nations Church
3617 Nina Court
Loganville, GA 30052**

johnenlow@mindspring.com
johnny@refugetothenations.com
www.refugetothenations.com

Printed in the USA
CPSIA information can be obtained
at www.ICGtesting.com
LVHW042312251023
762184LV00004B/66